The Adventures Of Gray Wolf

DON BUTCHER

NUSHATOGAINI
PRESS

For a personalized, autographed copy of this book, mail a check or money order for $20.00 post paid (along with the person's name) to:
Don Butcher
3819 Old 27 South
Gaylord, MI 49735

For information, address:
Nushatogaini Press
4603 Pinehurst Ave. S.W.
Wyoming, MI 49548
www.nushapress.com

Second Nushatogaini Press Edition: October 2002

ISBN 0-615-11922-0

PRINTED IN THE GREATEST AND FREEST COUNTRY IN THE WORLD,
THE UNITED STATES OF AMERICA.

I am dedicating these memories to my wonderful wife and partner in life for the last 59 years—none other than Edythe. Without her love, patience, and understanding, a great deal of my adventures would not have happened.

Edythe or "Shorty" as I call her, knew from the very beginning my great love for the outdoors and has always understood when I go on my fishing and hunting trips.

I love her very dearly and publicly want to thank her for making my life as pleasant as it has been. Thanks again honey for being you, and for your love and understanding of me and my wanderlust.

ACKNOWLEDGMENTS

This book of memories was prompted by Jeff Wenzel, one of two sons of some very dear friends of ours, Denny and Carol Wenzel. In the early 1980s, I flew the four of them to our camp in Canada for their first adventure of fishing in the Canadian Bush Country. They were all thrilled and we had a great time together. We caught lots of fish and told lots of stories of previous happenings in our lives. As a result of this trip the Wenzels were hooked on Canada and I found them a nice cabin on the Montreal River, about 40 miles southwest of our camp in Ontario and they purchased it.

It was Jeff that talked me into putting some of my adventures down on paper, hence the following from me to you. Thanks Jeff for your persistence in motivating me to recall some of my fondest memories.

– Gray Wolf

To my good buddy Gray Wolf,

I'm not sure who said it, but "Good things come to those who wait." After six long years it's finally finished. I looked back at the first batch of memories you put on paper and the envelope is dated June 3, 1995—just 16 days before your plane crash at the Soo! Whoda' guessed that was about to happen? Only the Good Lord had a clue, and I thank Him for keeping you around.

I have thoroughly enjoyed compiling your stories and gettting them into book form. What a wonderful history you have to pass along to your family and the generations that will follow—not to mention the rest of us.

You're a good man Gray Wolf and as you always say, "There's darned few of us left!" I'm happy that our lives actually crossed paths in this vast world and we got the chance to wet a few lines together—my only regret was not having the chance to do it more often. Both you and Edythe will have a lasting place in my memory and in my heart.

God's greatest and continued blessing to you and your family.

•••

I would like to thank my wife Kendra for her unending love and patience over the many years we put this book together. A black cover?? I Love You.

– Jeff Wenzel

Contents

How I Became Known As Gray Wolf

As a result of an experience at our beloved Nushatogaini Lake in Ontario, Canada I was dubbed as Gray Wolf. It was the middle of October and six of us were up hunting moose. Some of the ponds were freezing over and it was a cold, blustery day—very windy with seasonal snow showers. We had a Piper Super Cub and my Super Cruiser airplane, and we had lucked out that trip and killed four moose. They were all bagged up and ready to fly over to Five Mile Lake Lodge. By taking out the back seat of my plane and installing a built up floor I could fly out a whole moose if it was not a real monster.

Bob Peterson, the other pilot, was a tall easy going person with a ruddy complexion. We dubbed him with the radio handle of Red Fox. We loaded my plane and I took off with the first load headed for Five Mile Lake.

The wind made it easy to take off, but there were a lot of thermals which made it hard work to keep the plane on level.

After unloading, I waited for Bob to bring in his first trip. After helping him unload, we both headed back for our second bunch of meat. It was about a twenty minute flight from Five Mile to Nushatogaini and flying empty we really got kicked around with updrafts from the rugged terrain we were flying over. The boys loaded Bob up for his second trip, and off he went. When I arrived the second time at Five Mile, Bob was already heading back to camp, so the lodge operator and I unloaded my moose and back I went to Nushatogaini.

By the time I got back to our lake they had the Super Cub all loaded, and Bob met me on the dock with a drink in his hand and said, "Boy, I am all pooped out fighting this wind. Will you fly my plane with the last load?"

Well, I was pooped too, but he was in no shape to fly, so I climbed into his plane, checked everything over and said to Bob, "How is your gas supply?" He answered, "No problem," so I started up the plane, taxied out and away I went. My plane is set up so that both fuel tanks feed at the same time, but with his Super Cub, you had to switch tanks when one got low.

I was flying quite a heavy load, and thank God I was flying what I call my "safety route" which has different lakes under me most of the time. I was flying about 1,000 feet above the ground and was within about 10 miles of Five Mile Lake when the engine all of a sudden stopped running!

Flying a strange plane, I can tell you I was really moving fast and furious trying to find the right valve to switch to his auxiliary fuel tank. All this time I had to put the plane in a forward dive to help keep up my air-speed. I quickly primed the engine, hit the starter and what a beautiful sound when that motor started! I climbed up over the trees and shortly afterward landed at Five Mile Lake.

After gassing up, I headed back to Nushatogaini a very tired fellow. After tying the plane up I really read the riot act to Bob, alias Red Fox. He just grinned and said, "Cool off old Gray Wolf, and you'll live longer."

Ever since that day my CB handle was Gray Wolf, and many of my close friends call me that too.

FOND BEGINNINGS

I attribute my love and knowledge of the great outdoors to my mother Bessie Butcher, who immigrated from Scotland to a little whistle stop of a town in North Dakota named Wimbledon. She came to the United States to help her sister take care of her young family. While living in Wimbledon, my mother met my father who also immigrated to the same spot to take the job as a depot agent for the Midland Continental Railroad. Wimbledon was the end of the line for the Midland, which worked with the Soo Line Railroad shipping grain, wool and cattle to other points of the country.

My dad lived in a converted boxcar for quite some time while the depot was being built. This was a rough, raw country in those days, namely the very early 1900s. Our water was hauled in by teams of horses and wooden tanks, as all the water close to us was alkaline tasting.

We used rain water for baths, dishes and other chores.

During the summers it was blistering hot—the country was flat as a pancake, and there were almost no trees for shade. In the winter it got to 40 and 50 degrees below zero, and we still have pictures showing the snow up to the cross braces of the telegraph lines!

Mother and dad were married and moved into the new depot in 1914. In June of 1916, my brother Arthur was born, and in November of 1919, Donald Thompson Butcher—now known as the Gray Wolf—made his appearance. I was born in a severe blizzard and my father went to get a neighbor woman to help. In the storm, dad lost his bearings and almost froze to death. He finally saw a lamp light, stumbled up onto a neighbor's porch and collapsed. A piece of his right earlobe was frozen so badly that it came away from the lobe, and never did grow back. It appears that I was a problem right from the start!

In 1928, things got pretty rough. We experienced a very bad drought, and all the crops were burned up by the sun. The tumbleweeds were the only things growing, and they too finally gave up. North and South Dakota got the name "The Dust Bowl" tagged on them, the cattle died and the dust and tumbleweeds took over the prairie!

Due to no shipping, the Midland Railroad was going out of business, which meant my dad would be out of work. He had a friend in Winnipeg, Manitoba who got him a job on the Winnipeg Stock Exchange paying $15 per week. Dad moved up to his new job and mother took over as the depot agent until the Midland shut down in 1930.

We moved to Winnipeg joining my dad, and shortly

thereafter the Stock Exchange closed up because of the Depression. Dad got a job working at the Hudson Bay Company in the shipping department at $18.50 per week, working his way up to what they called a floor walker, kind of like a foreman.

Right across from the Hudson Bay Company was a big building that formerly belonged to a head honcho of some brewery. The structure was three stories high, with a basement and a sub-basement. This was remodeled to an employee restaurant and recreation building for the Hudson Bay Company employees and my mother got the job as hostess. We in turn had the third floor for our living quarters plus a small salary for mother.

We lived there for about seven or eight good years. My brother Arthur and I took care of the grounds in the summer and stocked a huge wood burning boiler that was the heating system. That hummer took four-foot logs and really put out the B.T.U.s, not to mention many sore backs to us for keeping it fired up.

Some of the best days of our lives were spent while we lived at the Hudson Bay's Beaver Club. Things were very tight for money, but we all saved collectively for our dream of having a cabin on Gull Lake which was about 60 miles northwest of Winnipeg. It was a gem of a spot about five miles south of Lake Winnipeg. It was a smaller lake, about one and one-half miles long and maybe three-quarters of a mile wide, but it was situated just right for us, offering lots of good fishing and hunting with very few people around.

There were several self sufficient farmers in the area eking out a meager living for their families—depending on their crops, farm animals, gardens, and game and fish they took as needed. There was a small trading post on the west side of the lake that took farm goods in trade for staple groceries and clothing, and also for the few tourists that would brave the roads to get to this area.

My brother Arthur and I had the unique opportunity at the ages 12-1/2 and 10 respectively to spend the whole two months of July and August at our lake, living in nothing but a tent! Our folks would come up and visit us about every two weeks and bring us the staples to eat. We supplemented what they brought us with lots of fish and berries, and whatever else that we might acquire. We often traded fish for eggs and milk with one of the German farmers that lived about a mile away.

We had an old wooden boat and a pair of oars, and fished quite a lot. Our equipment was quite meager, consisting of a hand line and wooden plugs that we carved out of old broom handles. Arthur would row until I caught a fish and then I would row until he caught one.

It got quite cold at nights and we would heat rocks by the fire and wrap them in a blanket, and it worked quite well to keep us warm. Our refrigeration consisted of a deep hole in the ground with a wooden cover which we covered with moss. We learned many skills and became quite woods wise on how to snare rabbits, and also became quite good with our slingshots. Several times we would get a real thrill when a bear would come to investigate who was intruding on his home ground, but never did it occur to us that they might harm us.

We became very good friends with the Block family who were our closest neighbors, being the German family that farmed about a mile away. We often helped with any chores they had and in return would possibly get some fresh baked goods, or maybe a chicken, or some cured ham. We also chummed with another farmer at the south end of the lake named Kulbaba. They were Galician people that immigrated from Europe, and were homesteading their farm on some government plan that stated if they worked the place for so many years, it was then deeded to them by the Canadian Government.

Our minister from Winnipeg built a cabin about a quarter-mile from our campsite, and he would visit us quite often to see that we were OK. After camping like this for a couple of years we had saved $100, which was the cost of our lot on Gull Lake. We picked a beautiful spot about a half-mile from where our minister's cabin was and bit by bit, as we could afford it, we built our log siding cabin.

The farmers, our minister, mum, dad, Arthur and I built the whole cabin. It was 24x24 feet, consisting of two small bedrooms, a kitchen, living and dining room combined, and a front porch. Bit by bit we furnished it, with many donations from the employees of the Hudson Bay Company.

We used our cabin from spring break-up until freeze-up in the fall, and Arthur and I knew every inch of the woods for miles around. We jointly bought an older Remington .22 caliber pump rifle and both of us became very good shooters with it. Ammunition was expensive for us, so every shot had to count. We shot crows, and turned their feet in for a two and one-half cent bounty that I believe was sponsored by Ducks Unlimited. I had a friend at the Hudson Bay Company that would give me a box of shells for a brace of partridge or ducks, so we always had ammunition after this.

Intruders At Gull Lake

Two years after we built our cabin, we had an intrusion on our privacy as another family built another cabin right next door to us. They were nice people, but real dumb in the way of the woods! I will never forget the time that we were enjoying a nice feast of locally picked mushrooms and the neighbors came over and tasted them, and wanted to know where we had picked them. We told them right where to go, and they too came home with a nice bunch.

They were apprehensive as to whether they were OK to eat, so they cooked a few up for their dog and fed them to him with some hamburger. Not seeing any adverse effects on the dog, they cooked up the rest and really had a feast. It was a real hot day, and later in the day the neighbors came home and lo and behold their dog was lying on his back with his feet sticking right up in the air!

They panicked, thinking the dog was dead, and drove over 14 miles of corduroy road to the nearest town where they all promptly had their stomachs pumped! Back they came over the rough corduroy road, and as they drove into their yard they had their car lights on, and who was there to greet them? Right, it was their dog—he had only been sleeping in the sun on his back! We had many good chuckles over this incident.

The same neighbors had quite a bit of money and kind of looked down their noses at us poorer folks. We wanted to have a stone fireplace in our Shangri-la, but could not afford it at the time we built the cabin. We did frame up a base and poured it full of hand mixed concrete for when we could afford to build it.

Well, the day came and we cut the floor out and proceeded to build our fireplace. We went by a plan in a *Popular Mechanics* magazine and got hold of an old wagon wheel rim that we cut in two to form the arc of the fire box. We hand picked all the stones, and bit by bit it became a reality. After letting it cure, we lit it up and it performed beautifully.

The neighbors became envious of us and promptly hired some so-called experts to build their unit. When it was completed they touched off a fire and guess what—it smoked like the blazes. This couldn't have happened to a better bunch of snob noses. After several attempts to fix the situation, and many dollars later, it finally worked. We had many laughs over this incident too!

Our First Guns

Arthur and I scrounged and saved our money, doing odd jobs until we had enough to buy our first shotguns. Mine cost $12 and was a double-barrel Iver Johnson 12 gauge. Arthur bought himself a double-barrel Belgium gun that I still have in my possession. We became very avid duck hunters, and really had some great times together.

I remember that I thought I was such a good shot—and I was on rabbits, crows and partridge—but not with the first flock of blue bills that flew over in their migration. I held for the lead duck and knocked down one of the very last birds! This kind of deflated my ego, but also made me a better wing shooter.

Later in the fall, and not having a car, we would often walk the three or four miles to a little settlement called Begonia. It had a great marsh right off the south shore of

Lake Winnipeg. The ducks really poured into the marsh and we had it practically to ourselves.

I remember one night after dark we were walking home to our cabin with our day's bag limit. We were followed by some timber wolves that came too close for comfort, probably after our ducks, and really made our hair stand on end! We were a couple of scared kids that night! We would shoot into the dark when they got too close, but I am sure we did them no damage.

The Longest Winter

When Arthur graduated from high school he wanted to go to college, but our folks did not have the funds. One of the butchers in the Hudson Bay's meat department suggested and agreed to buy all of the frying chickens we could raise in the summer. We raised lots of Leghorn Fryers at our cabin retreat, and made enough money to enter Arthur into college where he majored in animal husbandry. We did this for two summers and all went well until the fall of 1935, when a great tragedy struck our family.

On October 4, 1935, Arthur and I got up real early and walked to our favorite marsh for a day of duck hunting as we had done many times. It was a butterfly day, nice and warm, and the ducks were not flying so good. So we started prowling around and found an old Indian wooden boat. It was not big enough for both of us to hunt from, so we took turns on a two-hour basis.

I had just finished my turn, and Arthur took my place in the boat. The last time I saw my brother was about 4 PM as he waved to me and went around a point of bull rushes. From time to time I heard his gun go off as he flushed some ducks, but he never came back to meet me.

I became quite worried and kept hollering for him, but no answer. I'll tell you, this 16 year-old boy grew up to be a man that night. I spent most of the night walking through the marsh hollering, hoping for an answer, but to no avail.

As it started to get light, I found the boat turned over on the other side of the marsh. In my anguish, I stumbled into the little settlement of Begonia and tried to get some help. My parents were notified and the whole town turned out to help me look for Arthur, but nothing was to be found.

The Hudson Bay Company really went overboard trying to help us. They paid for an airplane to fly back and forth over the marsh most of the following day, but nothing was found. There was an Indian settlement real close and they all tramped through the marsh in that cold water—even women in their bare feet—but again nothing. The Bay Company even rented us a cabin nearby, gave my dad a leave of absence and paid for all our needs while we continued our search.

We dragged the open water of the marsh, and on the third day I happened to bring up my brother's gun! It was fully loaded, which ruled out any possibility of a shooting accident. Even after freeze-up, we dragged and probed under the ice and again nothing. The Bay Company even used dynamite charges as sometimes they claimed it would bring up a body. Nothing.

We finally had to give up the search as the weather got too brutal. It was a sad, sad winter what was put in that year by all of us. As spring neared, the German farmers would check the marsh every day. On Mother's Day of 1936, as the ice went out, Arthur's body surfaced—and our long vigil had ended.

We will never know exactly what happened, and can only guess that probably reaching for a killed duck, he fell into the cold water and drowned even though he was a good swimmer. My mother temporarily lost her mind, but through the help of the good Lord, and friends and prayers, she fully recovered a short time later.

This incident just about ended my hunting career as dearly as I loved the sport. Through the efforts of both our minister Bob Frain, who was an avid outdoorsman, and my dear mother who knew how much I loved the outdoors, they convinced me that I should consider the incident the Lord's will and continue my outdoor activities. The next fall, our minister and I spent many days in the field together both hunting and fishing. Mum and I also spent a lot of time at our cabin, and she would also go out with me on many hunts.

Indian Joe

The next fall, my good friend Milan Kulbaba and I went goose hunting on an old muskeg area that had lots of little ponds on it. We stalked and killed several geese, and started home when it began to snow and turned into a real blizzard. The geese were holding us back, so we hid them in the grass and finally found our way off the muskeg to high ground. It was long after dark before we got back to the cabin and the women were just about ready to start a search party for us.

The next morning Milan and I went to get our geese, but they were gone—only a man's tracks in the snow, showing us where the person who had stolen our geese was headed. We followed the tracks for about three miles, and they turned into a log cabin that was occupied by the person we called Indian Joe.

He was a real loner, and everyone in the area stayed away from the man—either being scared, or not wanting to associate with him. Old Joe trapped, hunted, and fished off the land and didn't respect seasons or bag limits. Being only boys we were afraid of him, yet really mad that he had taken our geese!

We did get even with him sometime later, as we followed him and watched where he would put out his traps and snares. We lifted several fur bearers from his sets, and came upon a deer that had been freshly caught in one of his piano wire snares. We cut the deer in half, and took the loins and the hind quarters as repayment for our geese.

Old Joe was really mad and made all kinds of threats—but he couldn't prove who had done it, as others were quite capable of doing what we had done. We quietly considered it a kind of poetic justice.

The Incredible Mrs. Kulbaba

Milan's parents had a small homestead with a few cows and other farm animals. I remember coming home one night from a hunt and Milan's mother—who was pregnant at the time—was out milking the cows. The next morning I came to pick up Milan, and found that during the evening Mrs. Kulbaba had delivered her baby all by herself, and was back out milking the cows and doing other chores!

She thought nothing of this feat, as she claimed that back in the old country it was quite common for women to be working in the fields, go off by themselves and deliver their own baby, wrap it up, put the child on their backs, and go right back to working in the fields! I am sure that some mothers and children were lost by this practice, but they looked at it as just part of the way of life in those times.

The Great Bwana Hunter's First Deer

My first experience in Big Game Hunting took place back at dear old Gull Lake. Not being able to afford a rifle of my own, I borrowed a Winchester .30-30 from a friend and bought three shells for it. Milan and I were walking an old trail when three deer jumped up and ran in a semicircle behind us. By the time I could get the gun up, two of the deer had jumped across the trail. I swung on the third one—just like duck hunting—and lo and behold, it fell right on its nose in the snow, deader than a smelt!

Talk about beginner's luck! Boy, I was the Great Bwana Hunter when we dragged this deer home into our yard to show mum what great hunters we were!

MAKING DUE

The Hudson Bay Company closed up their employee's Beaver Club and sold the property, so consequently mother lost her job. We moved to an area called St. Vital, which at that time was on the very outskirts of Winnipeg.

I got a job delivering newspapers as a bonus route. This meant that the customers were very sparsely situated and covered several miles of territory. In the winter months I would cover this area on skis and put my trusty old take down .22 rifle along with me, and quite often came home with rabbits and partridge in my bag. I also set snares and we always had lots of rabbits for our meals, as well as for some of our friends who usually returned the favor by buying me some shells for my .22 or shotgun.

After graduating from high school it became necessary for me to help with the family finances, so I got a job working six days a week with the J.C. Wilson paper company unloading box cars of paper products. Looking back, I sometimes wonder if this is where I abused my back and am now paying for it. Oh yes, my pay for this effort was $18 per week, which was good for that time. If you went to the grocery store and spent $10 you could hardly carry it out in one trip!

I worked hard at my job and finally got promoted to head of shipping and receiving. This involved warehousing six floors of paper products, and being in charge of four other men who did the unloading, picking and filling orders, and shipping. I advanced to $25 per week salary, but I still dreamed of going back to the United States where a person could buy a brand new car for $600 F.O.B. Detroit.

In 1939, most of my friends were conscripted into the Royal Canadian Air Force, and after a short training session were shipped off to England where they suffered very heavy losses from the German Air Force. The Royal Canadian Police also took away the guns that I owned, as we were resident aliens to them! My father lost his job due to cutbacks in the labor force and moved down to Detroit, where he got a job and a room in Highland Park, Michigan.

Nearly all of my friends had gone to war and things didn't look too good for a future where I worked, so I quit my job, packed my belongings, and borrowed my first money—$100 from a bank—after one of the roomers my mother rented rooms to co-signed for my note. I moved to Highland Park with my dad and shared his room. I went out job hunting and was literally down to my last dime—and at this time for 10 cents you could get a combination bus and street car ticket, or a hamburger and coffee. I elected to walk in a southwest direction and look for a job as I walked home!

After walking about 15 miles since leaving home, I arrived in Hamtramck and went into a great big factory that had a help wanted sign on the door. After a quick interview I was offered a job at 60 cents an hour if I would go to work right then. I was kind of tired from my long walk, but went right to work. I spent eight hours of pure hell that night, cleaning up after everybody in a stinking factory.

After completing my shift I headed home and saw another sign saying 'Help Wanted'. In I went, and was offered the same thing—go to work right now and you are hired at 70 cents per hour. I dug right in and worked another eight hours, then went over to the first place, quit my job, picked up my check, and headed home! They just about had the police after me as I had been gone about 30 hours with no word from me!

Things went pretty good for me after that experience. I was a young man, kind of big and not afraid to work. The foreman took me under his wing and put me on a cutoff machine making bearings for cars. It was piece work, and I went right to work and started making pretty good money.

One day I saved the foreman's life. He was working right across from me and during the setup of a job, his shirt got caught in a twirling chuck and was drawing him right into the machine. I saw his facial expression of real fright and left my machine to run over to his—just as it was cutting into his belly!

From then on I was given the better jobs, and when they went into making aircraft bearings in a completely new building, I was given the opportunity to learn how to run a very large Warner & Swasey turret lathe. I learned fast and ended up with the best job in the factory, and was making really good money for those days.

Edythe Gould
The Catch Of My Life

Backing up a bit to the days of Gull Lake, I never had much time for girlfriends—they just interfered with my fishing and hunting. But just after we finished our cabin, mother invited a young lady by the name of Edythe Gould to spend some time with us.

Edythe was the daughter of mother's friends Olga and Howard Gould, who lived in Valley City, North Dakota. We often visited the Goulds when we would take the train from Wimbledon to Valley City.

My brother liked Edythe and they used to play together, but I always figured she was a spoiled brat—so I would go fishing on the Sheyenne River during these visits.

When I was informed that Edythe was coming to spend part of the summer at our cabin I wasn't too happy!

But lo and behold, when she showed up it was like a butterfly coming out of a cocoon—she had grown up to be a real beauty! I was growing up too, so nature took its course and we became quite interested in one another.

When she left that summer it was a sad occasion for both of us. We wrote quite often and we both thought an awful lot of one another. When I moved from Winnipeg to Detroit without calling her I was in the dog house—but I really at that time couldn't afford the phone call.

We exchanged many letters and phone calls, and the next summer—after mother, dad, and I had pooled our money and bought a home in Oak Park, Michigan—Edythe came to visit us.

Well, chemistry moved and we became engaged—and on December 6, 1942, we were married and bought a house in Ferndale, Michigan just north of Detroit. Gas rationing was on because of the war and I couldn't get time off as I was on deferment because of my job making crankshaft bearings for Pratt & Whitney aircraft engines. Our honeymoon consisted of a weekend in Pontiac, Michigan only 20 miles from our home!

This was a good time in our lives. I was making good money and we were living in a friendly neighborhood. In August, we were blessed by our daughter Donna Kay being born and she has done nothing but bring us great joy right to this very day!

North Dakota, October, 1944. On the left is my Father-in-Law Howard Gould holding our daughter Donna and his dog Pudge.

North Dakota Pheasant Hunt

In October of 1944, I received my final leave from the Army before leaving for the South Pacific. This was a sad time for us, knowing that when I left it was going to be quite some time before we would see one another again. Our daughter, Donna Kay, was only a year old and was too young to know what was going on.

While in Valley City, North Dakota my father-in-law who was an avid hunter, promised to take me pheasant hunting. There were so many pheasants that fall that the season was re-opened three times as the farmers threatened to poison the birds if the state would not cooperate and try to thin out the pheasants.

Our hunt took place in the Sheyenne River Basin. Howard's dog Pudge was a nice strong Spaniel and as we entered the first draw between two hills Pudge got real excited. As we followed behind the dog it seemed like the whole valley exploded. It was a big racket and I am sure over 100 birds got up all at once. I was so shocked that I just stood there and never fired a shot.

I was using Howard's Parker 12-gauge shotgun and it must have patterned a beautiful pattern because I ended up shooting three doubles along with a nice jack rabbit that morning. We limited out and were home in just over an hour. That was the first and last time for that type of hunting for me. Howard left that Parker to me in his will, and I still have it today, 57 years later.

Time flew and my furlough ran out, and after a tearful good-bye I was off to the South Pacific where I spent the next two years island hopping. The good Lord was with me and I was fortunate to return home to my loved ones. Many were not so lucky and did not make it. This was a time in my life that a person never forgets, and to this day I am still grateful to the good Lord who watched over us.

WWII
And The Return Home

The war kept getting worse, and after receiving three, six-month deferments from the draft because of my job, I answered the call to arms and joined the Army.

We were shipped to Fort Sheridan, Illinois for a short time, then loaded up like cattle on a troop train to Camp Barkley, near Abeline, Texas. There we took our basic training and I was hospitalized and operated on for a hernia. At that time you had to lie flat on your back for two weeks before they would let you walk.

Shortly after we went back to the live obstacle course under fire, both at day and night sessions. We received our first casualty when one of the men in our group panicked and stood up and was shot by machine gun fire. We went out on maneuvers and had mock battles with other groups. We were taught survival tactics and had long, forced marches with full field packs. Some of my friends from the hospital popped their hernias back out, and were returned to the hospital.

We were assigned to smaller groups known as Medical Supply Units. Our job was to get supplies onto the beachheads right along with the attacking forces, and to keep the supplies to the front lines. We were the only armed medics in the Pacific Theatre! We shipped out by train to Seattle, Washington and our first stop was Oahu, Hawaii. Here we took six months of jungle training and were back on the troop ships bound for—who knows!

We started island hopping after 34 days aboard ship—Einawatok to Mog-Mog, Iwo Jima, and Okinawa—eighteen months of hell. We never saw a town that was not blown to bits, and sometimes never having a payday for months at a time—which really didn't matter, as there was no place to spend your money anyway. The good Lord was with me, and I was one of the lucky ones that made it back home in one piece! My nerves were shot, and I couldn't even hold a cup of coffee without spilling it all over myself—but I was home!

We were scheduled to land in San Francisco, and stopped for fuel at Pearl Harbor. There was a strike on by the dock workers who refused to fuel or supply the ship, so we all—after spending eighteen months or more in combat—politely told them to move over, and we did the task of refueling and resupplying the ship. They were mad as hornets but did not want to tangle with a bunch of home bound G.I.s, and stood back and watched as we did the work.

Between Honolulu and California, our orders were changed and we were shipped through the Panama Canal to New York. From there we took the train to Camp McCoy, Wisconsin to be mustered out. We drew numbers, and within six hours four buddies of mine and yours truly were out of the Army!

Again, there was a bus strike on with only a few busses running. We were in a hurry to get home, so we chartered a taxi to drive us to Chicago. What a wild ride! This driver drove 70 to 80 miles an hour, and his lights went out so he drove in the dark the rest of the way! We all had been in many tight spots during the war, but that driver about scared the life out of all of us.

We arrived at the terminal only to find big lineups waiting to board the few busses that were running. I will always remember that Captain when he saw us service men all decked out with medals and hash marks for our overseas service. He put up his hand and said, "Everybody hold the line! These service men are in a hurry to go home!" and he let us board the bus ahead of everyone.

When I got back to Oak Park, I picked up my car that I had left for my dad to use and headed for North Dakota where Edythe and our little daughter Donna Kay were living with Edythe's parents. I drove the whole way without sleeping and it was a great feeling to be reunited with my loved ones.

In Valley City, I signed up for the 52/20 which was $20 per week for 52 weeks to help out the veterans while they got relocated and went back to work. Shortly afterwards we headed for Ainsworth, Nebraska where we picked up my wartime buddy, Vic Welke and his wife, and the four of us went on a scenic trip out West.

While enjoying the many things that Yellowstone

Park offered, we had to sleep in squad tents as everything was booked solid! This didn't go over too big with us, as we had just come from sleeping in the same kind of tents during the latter part of our overseas duty. Having to pay to sleep in the tents kind of rubbed us the wrong way, but what could we say—it was the only thing available! We spent about 10 days on the road, then headed back to Valley City.

A New Start & Cascaddin's Sheep Ranch At Hubbard Lake

After a short stay in Valley City, we headed back to our home in Ferndale, Michigan. I was welcomed back to my old job, but looking at the same old guys on the same machines I decided to say, "Thanks, but no thanks," and headed home. My old boss was quite concerned and said I was a fool and would starve to death, but I went home jobless.

My neighbor owned a feed, garden and pet supply store, and he offered me a job working with him for peanuts compared to what I could make in the factory, but I had made my choice, and Edythe backed me up (as she always does, God bless her!), and I started up on a new career.

The petshop business gave me a college education working with people from all walks of life. It was interesting but very hard work, especially unloading big semitrailers with 100-lb. bags of fertilizer. My employer, friend, and next door neighbor Stu liked to gamble and play the ponies, so he left the running of the store to myself and working partner Don Hunt.

Stu liked to hunt, and fixed it up so that I could go deer hunting with him at Hubbard Lake. This was a real nice setup. The property that we hunted on was like a thorn in the sides of some big hunt clubs, and Cass the owner warned us never to cross any fences into the club properties as we would likely be shot at! What a deal we had! For $50 we had the hunting rights, lived right in the farm house, and Mrs. Cascadden fed us royally—even fixing us lunches to take out.

I did not have a rifle at that time, so I took my trusty Remington Sportsman loaded with slugs. The first day, after seeing sixty or seventy does, along came a real nice buck all by himself. I took careful aim and touched off the shotgun, only to see my buck take off like a ruptured duck! I sat there mulling it over in my mind, and finally went over to where I had shot at the buck. I found lots of blood and trailed it about 50 yards down a hillside, and there was my trophy. It was a real nice nine-pointer, and after dressing it out I found it had been a perfect shot, blowing his heart into pieces.

Lesson #1: Always go and check the area over where you took the shot, and don't assume that you had missed your mark.

While at school in Manitoba I had studied taxidermy, so I mounted this rascal the old way—pickling the hide myself and building the neck over a two-by-four with excelsior and potters clay for muscles! It turned out real good, and even today he hangs proudly on our wall at the Eight Ball Club, which is our present hunting camp.

The following season, I was the proud owner of a brand new .300 Savage Model 99 rifle. Guns were still very hard to come by at this time due to the all-out war effort, but my mother had worked in a defense plant for several years and had a good friend working at Federal's store, and she managed to get the rifle for me.

I was hunting in a different blind that year, right next to some very private land. It was just breaking day when I saw something brown sneaking through the brush. Every once in a while I caught a flash of white and I just knew that this was my deer approaching. But as it got closer to me it was evident that I was wrong—it was the owner of the property we were hunting on, wearing a pair of brown Carhartt coveralls, with a white towel sticking out of his back pocket!!! I chastised him for taking such chances, but his comment was, "Who the hell would shoot me on my own land?"

Not long after this ordeal, I was settling down when I spotted a big black form sneaking through some alder bushes. Naturally I thought, "Boy—here comes a bear!", only to soon find out it was the owner's best friend wearing a completely black rain coat and a black skull cap! What a way to start the first day with my new rifle!

Shortly after this I was sipping on a cup of coffee when I spotted a nice doe coming toward me. Her tail was sticking straight out and another deer was right behind her with its neck stretched out sniffing at her. I slowly put my rifle up and scoped the deer, thinking that I saw spikes but was not sure. I let the two of them come a little closer and again I put the scope on the second deer. Sure enough, there were spikes on it. I slid the scope over and down to the heart area and touched my new prize off.

The doe scooted off and the buck jumped the fence right into the forbidden hunt club property that we had been told never to venture into! I sat there running all the events through my mind for a few minutes, then went over to the spot that the buck had jumped the fence, which was at the top of a big hill going down into the private land.

I was just about to cross over the fence because there was a good blood trail, when a voice boomed out, "Where the hell do you think you are going?" I told whoever it was my story and asked him if he had seen my buck and the reply was, "Yeah, I saw your buck. He slid down the hill and is laying right close to my blind. Come on down and I'll help you drag him up the hill!"

He was a very nice man who told me about the animosity between their group and Vern Cascaddin our host—but he also told me that if this happens again to come right to their club house and they would be glad to help out.

The next day I thought I would sneak hunt, and possibly drive something to my buddies. I sat until about 9 AM and started poking around looking for sign. I was on top of a big hill and looking down I could see the corner of our property. There was a thick patch of spruce right outside the fence line, and a good deer run coming from that direction.

About half way down I saw some movement in the thicket so I stopped, and after seeing nothing more, proceeded to sneak down the hill. When I was about a hundred yards from the corner I saw the movement again, only this time I was able to make out a hunter—and the darned fool raised his rifle and was pointing it directly at me!

I let out a war-hoop and ran right at him, only to find an older man with glasses that looked like the bottom of a Coke bottle. After letting him have it for pointing his gun at me like that, the hunter apologized, packed up his gear and said he would never come hunting again—because he was going to shoot at the movement, which happened to be me, without first being sure that what he was looking at was a deer.

Lesson #2: Always be sure of your target before trying to shoot it, and always be alert for your own safety!

I was not frightened until after the hunter had left and I sat down and thought about what had just happened—realizing that if I had not seen the man get up or had not hollered at him, that they could have been hauling me out of the woods. I went back to the farm house and did not go hunting for the rest of the day!

The following year I had lucked out and shot a nice six-point buck on opening day, and I was out pussy footing the hills trying to push some deer to my buddies. It was a beautiful sunny day and I suddenly got the urge to go to the bathroom. I looked around to find a fallen tree to sit on and found one right close to a big stump. Just a perfect place. I rested my rifle against the stump, took off my jacket and proceeded to drop my pants. I was thoroughly enjoying myself in the warm sunshine when I heard a rustle in the leaves and here comes a spike horn. He stopped behind the stump, not over 20 yards from me. So I picked up the gun but could not get a good shot at the buck in the position I was in—caught with my pants down! Boy, would I give a good sum for a movie like this. I raised up with my pants hanging down and shot the buck in the neck. He dropped right there and never even knew I was there.

On another occasion, I was sitting on the same hill that I mentioned before where the old man just about shot me for a deer. There was no snow on the ground and it was nice and warm. I hunkered down behind a stump just off a nice deer run and was really enjoying my surroundings when I heard a shot from the swamp at the bottom of the hill, then two more shots.

All at once I saw a movement and something was running towards me at a fast pace. It looked more like a dog than a deer, running all stretched out and close to the ground. It came straight for me and about 30 yards away it put on the brakes and wheeled to the left. When I realized that it was a nice buck, I quickly swung around and flipped a shot at him but he just kept right on over the hill.

After sitting there going over the experience, I waited a while then walked over to the spot I had shot at the buck—nothing, just tracks. So I followed them a bit farther and, sure enough, there was the start of a blood trail. I eased along slowly, and maybe a hundred yards farther on, there lay a five-point buck. How he ran so low to the ground I will never know. That deer was as surprised to see me as I was to realize that it was a deer, and a pretty nice buck.

We spent several seasons at Hubbard Lake and had great times. I remember my last hunt at the Sheep Ranch. It was November of 1947. My nerves were shot from service in the South Pacific. I could not lift a cup of coffee without spilling it on me, and could hardly make change at the pet shop without spilling some on the counter which was very demoralizing.

I had just come home from bowling that night and felt really bad. I told Shorty, my everloving wife, "I'm going to have a hot bath, pack, and leave for deer camp the next morning." I climbed into the tub and the walls started to spin round and round, so I called to my wife for help. Shorty heard me and came into the bathroom, and by then I had passed out and my face was in the water. She picked up my head and I came to, and started to vomit blood into the tub. I do believe the warm water saved my life. After sitting there for a while, I crawled out and went to bed. The next morning I got up, packed, and Stu Morley and I took off for deer camp.

It was opening day and after a while I decided to sneak hunt. I was coming along a bunch of planted pine trees when about 25 feet in front of me I saw movement

Stu Morley (left) and Gray Wolf, with two Shotgun Bucks from Cascaddin's Ranch.

and a deer started to get up. He stuck his head out and then finished standing up. I had seen that he was a buck, but could only see his legs and body. I followed up his right leg, moved a little higher and to the left, and touched off the old .300 Savage. The buck pitched forward and died on the spot.

I gutted it and wrapped a rope around his head, figuring I would drag him out to the road, but I was so weak from my own loss of blood that I could not drag him. Cass came along and helped me get the deer out, which I was very thankful for. The very next day Cass died tragically, which ended our hunting at Hubbard Lake.

Guinea Pigs & The Beginnings At Otsego Lake

After coming back from our last hunt at Cascaddin's I went to see Dr. Schunamam, and he gave me hell for going deer hunting after losing so much blood. It took me from December to May to build myself up to be strong enough for surgery. I checked into the Veteran's Hospital in Dearborn, MI to be operated on for duodenal ulcers. There were two other veterans waiting for the same operation. We were to be guinea pigs for treating this problem, and the Army flew three surgeons in from Chicago to operate on us.

One man had his stomach removed and they put in a pig's stomach. He lasted about three weeks and died. The next man had his stomach removed and replaced with a sheep's stomach. They removed two-thirds of my stomach, then pulled the intestine up and sewed it to my stomach. This is the only time in my life that I kind of gave up and really was ready to go to the Happy Hunting Land. But the good Lord was not ready for me, and gradually I gained strength and was released from the hospital about one month after surgery.

I watched my friend Jim, the second guinea pig, slowly get worse and he finally developed cancer and died shortly before Christmas. The doctors told us that I would be fortunate to live another year and to seek a less stressful life.

Edythe and I, along with my folks, decided to look for a resort which we thought would get us out of the rat race of suburban Detroit. We made many trips to Northern Michigan looking for somewhere that had good churches and schools, plus a hospital and shopping places. Otsego Lake, which is 3-1/2 miles south of Gaylord won out. Mum and dad sold their home and moved up in the fall of 1952. Edythe and I did the same thing in the spring of 1953. Both families pooled our resources and went into the resort business as partners. We all worked hard and really enjoyed what we were doing. There were a lot of adjustments in our way of living, but it all worked out very well.

Our budget was tight and dad and I had to learn to be plumbers, electricians, carpenters, and the like. The kids, Donna was nine years old and Butch was two and a half, really loved this life. It was hard on Edythe though. She cried herself to sleep for a long time, but before long we all enjoyed it. Because of my health we made many sacrifices, but it paid off in many ways. We were a closely knit family, willing to make due with what we had.

After a few months, our expenses were more than our income and I went to work at Standard Products, a factory which was close to home. Working from 3 to 11 PM gave me time to work all morning at the resort. When I got home from work, we would go to different spots gathering nightcrawlers to sell to the fishermen. I buried an old wooden ice box and kept the crawlers there. That was the start of Don's Sport and Marine Shop. Mum and dad would sell the crawlers while I worked at maintaining the resort and cleaning a good swimming area.

Our lake front was the site of an old saw mill and there were literally thousands of pieces of slab wood from the old mill buried in the sand. We paid our kids and their friends one cent a slab to drag them onto the beach and pile them up. Later, Don Huff and I used an old farmer's hay rake and a cable tied to my old Jeep truck, and we took out 14 five-yard truck loads of slabs—plus hundreds of Jeep loads before we had a good place to swim.

We built a shuffleboard, volleyball, and horse shoe area, and we have many pleasant memories of games with our guests. Our customers became like family and came back year after year to vacation with us. These were some of our best years, and our children—Donna and Butch—grew up in a pleasant atmosphere. Money was tight, but we always had plenty to eat and did things together.

From the money made on nightcrawlers I bought some basic hooks, spinners, bobbers, and crawler harness lures which were sold in mum and dad's vestibule. I cleaned out an old shed behind the folks' home and bought six horse tanks and started catching minnows to sell.

Bit by bit our inventory grew and I bought a couple

of old outboards, fixed them up and started renting boats. We put in an old gas pump and Edythe, mum, dad, and I all took turns selling to the fishermen. When we were not available, we left the door unlocked and people took care of themselves, leaving the money in a coffee can! Boy, you surely could not do this today! It wasn't long before I added on to the shed and started stocking whatever the fishermen wanted. We would put a tank in our old station wagon and drive to Grayling, Houghton Lake, and Alanson, to buy our minnows as the demand was more than I could trap.

Mum and dad's home was rather small, so we added on to it and installed a real nice Onoway stone fireplace. Our home started out as the place for Town Hall Meetings. We have been told that it is one of the oldest buildings on Otsego Lake. We have added on to this, and made a real comfortable three-bedroom home. We also added porches to our three lakefront cottages, and built a new double-unit between our home and the lake. We did all this in the fall, and I would keep my shotgun handy, and shot quite a few ducks for the freezer.

We catered to deer hunters in November and were always full for the last two weeks in November. I acted as a guide for some, and buddy hunted with others. I hunted every day and was fortunate to keep our freezer stocked. We always had big doings for all of the hunters, which was sponsored by the Chamber of Commerce. Much fun was had by all, and prizes were given to some of the lucky hunters.

The first year we catered to deer hunters, Arnie Pawlitz (who used to deliver supplies to our pet shop in Ferndale) came to hunt with us. His record was 11 years

Above: Dad at the break of day on Otsego Lake.

Left: Mum with a big perch, also on Otsego Lake, 1956.

of hunting with no deer. He also failed to get a buck that year, but shot a small spikehorn in his 13th year of hunting. We still kid him about shooting a goat! The following year Arnie brought up his two bosses, Ray and Wayne Pelton, along with another pet store owner, Hank Johnson. They rented our largest cottage, which was Kozy Cottage, and they returned year after year. We all became real good buddies and spent many years hunting together.

A smiling Arnie Pawlitz and his "goat". It was the first deer he had shot in thirteen years of hunting.

Gray Wolf, cleaning ducks shot on Otsego Lake while working on our lakefront cabins.

Donna's first deer at 16 years old.

The Horicon Hunting Club

I worked out a deal with a very large club called the Horicon Club. We would patrol their property and in return, we had the right to hunt the northern part for ourselves. We hunted this property for many years with good success.

Our daughter Donna became an avid hunter and we sat together in my old stump blind where she shot her first deer, making a clean kill. I showed her how to gut the deer and she did it by herself. All the gang came over to congratulate Donna on doing such a good job. While this was going on I drove home and picked up our movie camera. I went back, and we put the guts back into the deer and had Donna do it all over again on film! We still get more chuckles out of this episode. When our son Butch became 14 years-old we built him a stick and stump blind, and he shot a nice spike-horn the second day of the season.

One year Hank brought his brother Jerry to hunt with us. Jerry was dressed in an all bright yellow hunting suit—boots and hat too! He looked like a light bulb and we all razzed him saying, "A deer wouldn't come within a quarter-mile of him, decked out like that." We were all wrong. Jerry saw lots of deer and shot a really nice buck. One never knows, do they?

The next season Arnie brought his cousin Jim to hunt with us, and he was a real character. The second morning it was snowing quite hard, and Jim had a nice 6-point buck trot by close to where he was sitting. Jim emptied his gun at the buck and hit it twice. He was so excited that he put his gun down and took out after the buck. After a while he found the deer and gutted it out, only now he was totally lost. Being a young man, he grabbed the antlers and started dragging the deer. He finally found a road and sat on the deer without his rifle, but still had his hunting knife.

After some time, a friend of mine came along in his car and stopped to see if he could help. Jim told him that he was hunting with me, but did not have any idea where he was. Lucky for him the man knew where I hunted, and drove Jim and his buck back to our area. It was about 1-1/2 miles as the crow flies, but almost six miles driving because he could not cross the private hunting club. It is not every day you drive up on someone sitting on a freshly killed buck with only a hunting knife as a weapon.

Another year Donna and I were hunting in our stump blind at the Horicon Club, and her husband Robert King went to a spot at the base of some hills that was one of my favorite spots. Some time in the early afternoon we heard four shots from where Bob was supposed to be. After waiting a bit we decided to go see what had happened. We came across a good blood trail in the snow with Bob's tracks following it, so we naturally followed them too. After maybe a couple hundred yards, another man's tracks joined the blood trail with Bob's. We soon came to a pile of guts, still steaming, but no deer!

About this time POW!, then we heard, "I got him for you," so we continued on and came across Bob and my hunting buddy Frank Tozser. They were down in a pothole and were in the final stages of cleaning Bob's buck out.

What had happened was four deer came bounding off the hill where Bob was, and the last one was a nice six-pointer. Bob shot four times as they ran across a clearing, and he was sure that he had hit the buck at least once. His shot had creased the buck across the belly, and as the buck ran the wound opened and his intestines dropped out. The buck stopped and somehow stepped on the intestine, and everything behind the diaphragm dropped out in the snow—hence the gut pile we came upon. Still having his heart and lungs held in by the diaphragm, the buck continued to go and headed for the pothole that had some water in it to cool him off. That is where Frank found him standing in the water and shot him. It's hard to believe that any critter would have the stamina to do this, but believe me it happened just the way I told you.

The next day I crawled into what I call my fallen tree blind. The tree had blown over in a wind storm and after some modifications with my trusty little axe, I made a great place to hunker down against using the uprooted roots as my back rest.

It was a beautiful, sunny day and I noticed a beautiful buck coming from the northeast walking directly towards me. I just sat still and let him come! He came to a road about 75 yards from me, stopped, looked things over, then turned around and started to walk back the same way he came. He did not give me much of a shot—only his rear end—but he was such a beauty that I scoped him, and touched off the old .300 Savage and the darned deer just disappeared.

I crawled out of my blind and walked over to where I thought he could have been, but no buck. By this time my hunting partner Arnie came over to see what had happened. Arnie stayed there while I crawled back to the blind and recreated what had taken place. In my excitement I had gone too far to the left, so I waved Arnie over to the right and he hollered, "Come over here!" So over I went and there was lots of blood and knuckle bone from the back leg.

We followed the blood trail for maybe 75 yards, and there among some newly planted Christmas trees lay my buck and a beauty it was too—a perfectly formed 8-pointer. I had hit him right where I had aimed hoping to break his back, but the bullet had deflected down from the hip joint and castrated him. It took only a short time for him to bleed to death, so he did not suffer very long. Today his mounted antlers are still on the wall in my office at home, constantly reminding me of the great times of the past.

One of the last hunts at The Horicon Club involved our son-in-law Bob King, Smoky Beaulieu—a school teacher from Gaylord, and myself. It was a beautiful, crisp morning and the rising sun made it look like sparkling diamonds on the new fallen snow.

I was following a nice fresh track and came across a buck rub on a tree, and the bark was laying right on top of the snow. I whistled, and Bob and Smoky took up the fresh track that was heading up to the top of a range of hills and thicker cover. I stayed down on the flats moving real slow, hoping that they might spook the buck out to me.

The flats ran from the hills about a quarter-mile to some real thick brush around the south end of Tecon Lake. They were void of trees and covered with very large white pine stumps that dated way back to the lumbering days of the late 1800s. I hunkered down with my back against one of the big stumps thoroughly enjoying the beautiful sunny morning, knowing that Bob and Smoky would eventually come out close to my spot as it was the south end of the club property.

The shore of the lake at the south end was quite brushy and there was a cement dam about three feet thick to control the lake level. I selected a spot about 100 yards from the hills and hunkered down so I could watch the hills. It was not very long before several does came running down from the hills and ran across the stump field into the brush at the end of the lake. The trees on the hillside were all covered from the snowfall the previous night. They were a beautiful sight.

I could hear Bob and Smoky as they started to descend down the hills, then all of a sudden a real nice buck trotted out and headed across the stump field following where the does had crossed. I took a shot at him but missed, and he shifted into passing gear—all stretched out and running low to the ground.

After giving me a good ribbing for not killing the buck, we figured he must have taken refuge in the brush because I had not seen him cross the cement dam to get to the west side of the lake. I positioned myself out in the stumps where I could watch the east side of the lake while Bob and Smoky would filter through the brush and flush him out to me.

We thought we had him trapped! As they poked around in the brush, probably 10 or 12 does popped out—two or three at a time—and came so close to me I could have hit them with a long stick, but no buck. None of us could believe this, so all three of us back tracked through the brush. We soon found where Smoky had walked within 20 feet of where that old buck had lain in the snow—all stretched out with his head and neck pushed right down into the snow.

After Smoky had walked past, the buck got up and pussy footed right across the cement dam to safety on the west side of the lake. Boy, did he make a monkey out of us! We never attempted to chase the buck any longer as he deserved to live and pass on his craftiness to future bucks. Hats off to a real clever buck, and may he live to a ripe old age!

Our son Butch inherited the love of the great outdoors from his Grandma Betty and me. He started out with a bow and arrow, then graduated to a BB gun. He became quite a good shot—unfortunately even to shooting out some of the neighbors porch lights and windows. After a good lecture and taking the gun away from him for a while, he replaced the windows from his allowance and apologized to the neighbors. He learned that there were lots of things to shoot at, but there were also lots of things you had to respect.

Butch accompanied me on a lot of my trips into the woods and quickly learned how to hunt rabbits, pheasants, ducks and also deer. He used to read stories about trapping and bought himself traps and a trapper's basket. His sets for muskrats got better all the time and he even caught a couple of mink. It provided him with good wholesome time outdoors as well as a few dollars from the furs he sold. He did catch a couple of fox and I got permission from a friend of mine to trap beaver on his property.

We hauled the traps and gear about a quarter-mile into the swamp where Butch set his traps. The following day we went back, and lo and behold there was a beaver about 30 pounds in his trap. That same beaver, after lugging him back to the truck, must have weighed 130 pounds! We decided that was too much work, so that was the end of his beaver trapping.

When Butch was 14 years old I bought him a .30-30 Winchester lever action Model 94. He practiced and became a real good shot. That deer season we went to my favorite spot at the Horicon Club and built him a stick blind just over the hill from where I hunted. He saw several does and then along came a nice spike-horn buck, and he killed it with a nice, well placed shot right through the heart. Boy, he could not have been prouder if it had been a 10-pointer. I was just as proud to see that he had been taught well and knew what to do at the time of the kill, dressing out the buck in a real professional manner.

Donna's Trip Through The Valley

Back in 1970 our daughter Donna came down with a very serious and life threatening situation. It was not cancer but very similar. Thanks to Harold Elgas, the head of our local Cancer Society, Louis Arnfeld of Mt. Sinai Hospital and several notable doctors around our great country, they came up with a new blend of chemotherapy. Donna's doctor in Mt. Pleasant, Michigan had to be instructed on just how to administer this new blend of chemo, and so the process of hope, skill and prayers went into action.

This was a very traumatic time for all of us to see our beautiful daughter go through this ordeal. The treatments would make her very sick, she lost all of her hair and looked like a small monk for quite some time. The Man Upstairs was also very much involved and over time Donna gradually improved. Her hair came back to normal and it was like watching a beautiful flower blossom as she recovered. That was over 30 years ago and we are very grateful for this miracle to have happened.

Donna today is the picture of health, has a Doctor's degree in Biology and teaches at Central Michigan University. Donna and her sister-in-law, Louise, have opened a Beaver Boatique on Beaver Island, Michigan and have done very well with their project. The store stays open with the help of local employees from May through December. Donna could not have children as a result of her illness, and in lieu of them she and her husband Bob (who also has his Doctorate in Biology and also taught at CMU) have 25 beagles which they travel all over the country with to Field Trials. Two of their dogs are National Champions! This is a lot of work but the love every facet of it. Can you imagine being a grandparent to 25 beagles?

Donna and Bob are very active in their small Methodist church in Winn, Michigan, so you see that Donna was spared for a good reason—to help others. We are very grateful that her health problems turned out so well and are so proud of her accomplishments to date. Red Skelton said so often, "May God bless," and He certainly has!

Moose Hunt At Mile 122-1/2 Algoma Central Railway, Ontario

I believe it was in September of 1960, that I was invited to go moose hunting with the game keeper of a very large and private club. His name was Herb Townsend and we later became friends. Herb also invited another buddy, one of our local eye doctors, to go along too.

Herb owned a cabin up in Ontario, Canada that could only be reached by riding the Algoma Central Railroad. It was about three miles from the track at mile post 122-1/2 by the Black Spruce River. This was quite an honor and was to cost about $250. The license was at the time $101 and you could shoot either sex of moose, plus bear, wolf, and small game. The season started on September 15, which was ideal as it fell right in rutting season and the bulls responded to calling very well. My mother, bless her heart, helped me with the finances of my share, as money was real tight in those days.

This was to be the "hunt of a lifetime" and would probably happen only once in my life. As it turns out I have gone moose hunting for 30 years and have legally shot 33 of them. I carried all of them out of the woods and have enjoyed eating every last morsel! Moose meat in my opinion is better than beef and much better for you. All of our family loves it as do many of our friends.

Well, little did I know what I was getting into, as my three partners were quite the bottle tippers and I was a tea-totaller! The day of our hunt finally came, and the four of us with all our gear headed for Canada. We had to spend the night at Sault Ste. Marie, Ontario because the train left at 8 AM the next morning.

The boys got feeling real good that night and finally got to bed around 1 AM. The next morning I got them up in time for breakfast and it was the first time I had ever seen anyone crack three eggs in a glass of tomato juice and drink it as a stimulator!

The Algoma train is amazing. It will stop anywhere it is flagged down—which could be to drop off a bull-dozer, or a pack of needles to some Indian squaw and still keep a pretty good schedule. Finally the train stopped at mile post 122-1/2 and we got off with all our gear.

We had to walk about a quarter of a mile to an old shed that Herb had a real old Jeep parked in. After an hour of tinkering with the Jeep and pushing it down a hill it started, and after about three trips in and out we finally got into his cabin with all our gear. The Jeep always had to be parked on a hill to help start it! The cabin was rustic but very functional and water was taken from the lake or creek for dishes, cooking, and bathing. Herb and Dick Bentz were the cooks and we ate very well.

Opening morning we were up and on our way to the areas we wanted to hunt. I teamed up with Dick Bentz who had hunted the area before. I must say, he liked his drinks before the hunt and at night—but during the day it was taboo and he was an excellent hard working hunting partner. We basically walked old timber trails from lake to lake, stopping to listen and occasionally calling. Dick had a pump .30-06 and I was using my trusty .300 Savage.

About three or four miles from camp we approached a small lake with a real nice marsh on the north end of it. There we stood and two nice moose were about 200 yards away. We snuck up so that we could get a good rest to shoot from and I was to shoot at the young bull and Dick would take the cow. After two shots my bull dropped into the marsh grass and the cow was still running away, so consequently we both ended up killing the cow.

Dick knew where an old canoe had been hidden in the brush from other trips, so we dragged it out and prepared to get our two moose. The canoe was probably 15 feet long and was canvas-covered of cedar construction. It had a big bump on one side where it had been punctured and repaired with canvas and pine pitch. This made it awfully tippy to ride in, but we managed to paddle up to the marsh and located the cow, but found that my bull was still alive. He staggered up on his feet and got in the water, when I dispatched him with a shot to the head.

This is where the work begins. They are a big animal and you almost have to crawl into the chest cavity to get the heart, lungs and wind pipe out. We finally got them both field dressed and put sticks in their chests to keep them open to cool off properly. It was a happy camp that night, but we went to bed early as we had a job before us to get the meat out the next day.

We were up early, equipped with knives, a meat saw, moose cotton to wrap the parts in and Canadian bush packs to carry the meat. We skinned the moose where they lay using the hide as a cutting sheet to help keep the meat clean. We then cut them up into eight pieces, each piece being placed in a tubular type of breathable cotton which we tied at one end, put the meat inside, and tied again at the top. This keeps the meat nice and clean and serves as a bag to hang the meat from on a ridge pole back at camp.

It took us most of the day to pack it all out using old logging trails and crossing two lakes, but the effort is worth the work for that delicious meat. Of course, we had moose tenderloins that night and we also cooked the heart and tongue in spice water. This makes delicious sandwiches along with a big slice of onion!

Herb shot a small bull about a half-mile from camp which made the processing much easier, and that same day, Charlie shot a real nice bull right on one of the logging trails about a mile from camp. We were even able to use the old Jeep to haul this one back to camp—a real piece of cake!

We spent the next couple of days relaxing and fishing for pike and lake trout. We had great weather all week, and after several trips hauling our moose and gear out to the railroad we sat down and waited for the train to pick us up.

Herb had a red flag on a stick which he waved at the engineer and they stopped the train and backed it up so that the baggage car was right by our gear. With the help of a couple of the train crew we loaded up our moose and gear and headed back to Sault Ste. Marie, Ontario. There in the railroad parking lot were our car and trailer which we carefully loaded, and then headed back to Gaylord, about 110 miles south. What a trip.

Left to right: Gray Wolf, Herb Townsend, and Charlie Grimes with a nice bull from the Black Spruce River area of Ontario, 1960.

My Most Memorable Moose Hunts

This was to have been a hunt-of-a-lifetime-one-time-only deal, but before we got home we had our next year's hunt already planned. We went back about 10 or 12 times and were lucky enough to fill our tags 100% each year. I won't elaborate on each hunt as most of it would be too repetitious, but I have to tell of a few experiences that stand out from the normal hunt.

Out in the bush, there were a lot of partridge and spruce hens that were not spooky at all. In fact, they would walk in the trails right in front of us, or sit in the trees not at all afraid of us, so I always carried a sling-shot and a bag of marbles and rocks. I was able to shoot a lot of birds that we ate in camp and brought some home as extra goodies.

We usually had to cross a small lake that we called

Pike Lake, and as we crossed the lake we rigged short lines on three or four sticks about three feet long with a single hook and sucker minnows attached. When we came home after the hunt, it was great fun looking for our sticks. As we approached the stick with the canoe, it would stand up like a big bobber and go scooting away from us. When the fish got tired, we grabbed the sticks and hauled in the pike which we usually ate for supper.

When we shot a moose we would dress it out, prop open the cavity with a stick or two and place spruce boughs over the cavity to keep the ravens and Canada Jays from eating the tenderloins. Thinking back it was strange, but we never lost any meat from animals except once to wolves and that was in a different part of Ontario and another story altogether.

We always went back the next day as the meat would cool off by then. A big fire was built and quite often we would roast the heart on sticks over the fire and cut it up for sandwiches right on the spot. Boy, that was delicious. The four of us would skin out the moose, cut it up and bag it in stockinette, and pack it out on our backs in pack-sacks that were designed for such work. Each sack had a tump strap built right on the bag, which was adjusted so you could lean into the strap with your forehead to take some of the weight from your back and shoulders.

In an effort to save our backs while packing meat we bought an outfit that was mounted on a bicycle frame. It had a wheel in the center with a canvas affair, similar to a camp cot on top, and two handles both front and back. Dick and I had shot a moose a long way from camp so we took our new pack-out rig the next morning to make our job easier. After loading two hind quarters on the rig, we started home. Boy did this seem great! And it was, until we had to go down a very steep hill.

I was in front and Dick had the rear, and it had rained the night before so the trail was slippery. Well, you guessed it—we both lost our footing at the same time, and the darned rig loaded with moose meat ran right over me and ended up in the brush. Luckily it did not break any bones, but it bruised me up a lot. That was the end of our meat toter. We ended up using our bush bags, and for all I know the meat toter is still up there in the bush where we left it. If anyone ever finds it they will be looking for evidence of where it came from and who left it!

A full pole of moose meat back at camp, all bagged up and ready to fly home!

My Trophy Moose

I saw a picture in one of the sporting magazines of a man who had shot a huge moose and had his picture taken with his rifle across the antlers. I told my wife Edythe that I was going to get my picture taken exactly like that the next season.

The first day of the season I was walking on an old logging trail along a creek bed. It was just getting light and the morning mist was slowly rising when I heard a kind of sucking noise—just like pulling your foot out of some wet mud. I stopped to listen and again I heard that sound ahead of me. Slowly I snuck forward and suddenly about a hundred yards ahead of me I caught a glimpse of a dark body, and a large rack of antlers. He was my dream moose right out in the open in a small marsh just off the trail I was on. My heart really started beating with excitement and the moose didn't even know

I was there.

I crept up closer, and when he turned broadside to me about 75 yards away, I touched off the old .300 Savage where I figured his heart should be. To my surprise the moose did not even flinch—it just stood there—so I shot again for the same area. This time the moose turned around and then turned back to where he was when I originally shot.

About this time I was really shaking, so I laid down and shot again—this time from the prone position. My bull started to sway a little bit and shook his head, and then let out a big whoosh and dropped to his knees. I ran up the trail but could not hold my gun steady, so I rested it against a birch tree and sat down.

By this time the moose tried to get up again, but fell down in a heap. I sat there for a few minutes ready to pop him again but he was dead. There I was all by myself with an absolutely huge bull moose. After crossing the small creek, I walked over to admire my trophy and he was a dandy with a 54-1/2 inch spread on the antlers. He is the same moose that graces the front cover of this book.

Later on the next day I had my picture taken, just like the one I had seen in the magazine, with me standing by the moose and my rifle laying across his antlers. Even today, some forty years later, one of the outfitters I know still uses that picture in his brochures.

Well, now I had to field dress the rascal. We always carry a long piece of nylon rope in our packs just for this project, so I cut a hole through the hide of the bull's back leg and tied the rope there. I then went over to a tree a short distance away to pull the one leg out, exposing the underside of the moose. It is quite a job for one person to do alone, but I had lots of time and cleaned the body cavity out real good.

I always carried a small marble axe in my pack, and that was what I used to split the itch bone. Next I cut a spruce tree and made a stick to keep the cavity spread open. I cut the big tongue out, and went to get the heart but it was all shot to pieces. You could cover my three shots with the palm of your hand, but the .300 Savage just does not have the shocking power to knock such a big animal down with a heart shot.

Just as I was getting ready to go back to camp I heard two shots in the direction of where my partner was hunting, so I headed in that direction. After walking about a half an hour I came across Dick dressing out a nice bull with a 48-inch spread—so there I was into the blood and guts again, helping him field dress his moose. By the time we got back to camp it was late afternoon and we were really pooped. You might know it was a happy camp that night!

Wayne, The City Hunter

We had a new man in camp that year who was decked out in brand new hunting clothes. We hunted in khaki field jackets and pants as they were tough, blended into the surroundings, and were pretty waterproof. Wayne was what we called a "city hunter"—all decked out real pretty, and almost afraid to step into the mud or water. He always commented on how he would sure catch hell from his wife if he were to get dirty. A little of this went a long way, so we cooked up a scheme to take care of this situation.

When Dick and I went out to pack our meat from our bulls, we packed two bundles of liver and spleen into the back and bottom of Wayne's pack. We also cut several extra slices into the liver and spleen so that it would bleed real well.

It was at least a mile back to camp through muddy

trails and some swampy areas. We told Wayne this was the shortest way back to camp. Well, you guessed it, by the time we got back to hang the sacks of meat, he was a total mess—all muddy, and his whole backside had *somehow* gotten soaked in blood! He soaked his pack sack, jacket and pants in the river, but I do believe that to this day the stains still show. After this treatment, we never heard another word about what his wife would say and Wayne became a good hunting partner!

Runaway Freight Train

On another beautiful day I was hunting all by myself, walking a narrow old trail that was in real hilly country. On my left was a hill almost straight up and on my right was a deep ravine. All of a sudden I heard a bull grunt across the ravine on another hillside. I could not see the moose yet, so I called a real soft cow call. He grunted again and started coming down the big hill towards another trail that joined my trail about 200 yards ahead of me.

The bull would stop and listen, and every time I called he would grunt an answer and came further down the hill. Pretty soon I saw the bushes move and could hear him coming real well. He finally jumped down on the trail and looked around to see if he could spot the cow, which in reality was me!

The bull was a good sized animal and wanted to make

love. The distance across the ravine was about 100 yards, so I shot at him and down he went. I was wearing my regular tan hunting clothes but had a bright orange hat on. The bull got up and let out a real bellow and started running down the trail towards where it intersected with my path.

He came to a blown down tree across his path and as he jumped it I shot again and down he went a second time. I started to slowly walk to where the two trails came together, when the darn moose got up again and ran to the intersection. I thought he would keep going straight ahead, but instead he wheeled into my path and came straight at me with his head down and grunting. I was not too alarmed, but could not get off the trail to my left as it was all rock and to my right was the steep valley. I guess I just automatically pulled up the old .300 Savage and shot.

It was like a ton of rocks falling on him. His legs buckled and he skidded to a halt no more than 10 feet from where I was standing! I just stood there looking at the moose with those big antlers, and all of a sudden I started shaking so bad that I had to sit down and thank the good Lord that this episode ended as it did. The moose was no doubt hurt from my first two shots, and mad. He probably saw my orange hat as what was hurting him, so he charged me. I will never know what really happened, but from then on I used my .300 Savage for deer hunting, and take my Winchester Model 70, .30-06 when I go moose hunting.

I believe this episode was one of our last trips to Mile 122-1/2 on the Algoma Railroad/Black Spruce Area, as Herb's health was not too good and he was forced to sell his camp. Herb died two years later and our foursome changed as did our hunting area.

MOOSE HUNTS WITH LEE COLE'S FLYING SERVICE

After Herb died, we lost our good hunting buddy and a place to hunt, so the following year we made arrangements to hunt with Lee Cole's Flying Service which is located about 30 miles south of Chapleau, Ontario. Dick, Charlie, myself, and Dale Johnson —a Marathon Oil distributor—loaded all our gear in a covered trailer. Using Dick's new Ford we headed for the Canadian bush country. It is about a 300 mile trip and takes about six hours of steady driving. We left around 4 AM and after having breakfast at St. Ignace, Michigan, and lunch at Aubry Falls, we arrived at Cole's camp around 1 PM.

After loading the Beaver aircraft we took off for Bragh Lake. About 20 minutes out we started hearing a strange grinding noise. The pilot could not locate where it was coming from and he was really sweating it out—

thinking it was something wrong with his plane. After about another 10 minutes we landed and taxied up to our tent camp—our home for the next seven days. As we were unloading our gear we located the grinding noise when we opened Charlie's bag. Of all things, he had put in a battery operated pepper grinder! Boy, did he catch it from the pilot!

Our camp was a small squad tent with just enough room for our four sleeping bags and duffle bags. Charlie and Dale took the boat and brought us a few pike which we had for supper. We straightened up camp and built some shelves for our pots and pans, and cut some spruce poles to make a real handy cooking area. This we covered with a tarp and we were all set—comfy as four bugs in a rug.

We turned in early, as the next day was the opener of moose season for non-residents. It was a clear, crisp night and the stars hung like bunches of grapes. It seemed like there were millions of them and in the distance we could hear a cow moose calling, which really got us worked up.

After a big breakfast, Dick and Charlie took one of the boats and headed for the east side of the lake which had a nice marshy area. Dale and I took the west side which was brush covered and more hilly. About an hour after day light we heard two shots, then shortly after that three more shots. We heard a lot of hollering, so we went back to the lake—and here came Dick and Charlie just like two kids.

The first two shots were Dick's and he killed a nice bull. When they went over to gut it out, out came a bigger bull which Charlie knocked down with his second shot, and finished it off with a third one. We all went back to camp to get our block and tackle, axe, and saws—then back to the chore of cleaning the moose.

This set things up for the next day's work of cutting up the animal and hanging the quarters from a meat pole we had made. That night we had moose tenderloins smothered in onions, fried potatoes, a nice salad, creamed corn, fresh bread, and O'Keefes Ale. What a feast!

The next morning Dale and I were out at the crack of dawn and were following a small stream when we heard a cow call, and she was answered by a grunt from a bull. This was all new to Dale, as it was his first experience moose hunting. We crouched in the tall grass and I took my birch bark horn that I had made the night before and I gave a real seductive cow call. Then I took the horn and filled it with water and let it dribble back into the stream—making a sound like she was urinating in the water. This got the bull all excited.

You could hear him grunt and breaking brush coming off the hill. Every time he would stop, I would break a stick or two and splash my hands in the water to sound like a moose walking. All at once, a bull stepped out on a point of land about 50 yards away looking for a cow. Dale got all excited and wanted to shoot it, but I told him to wait as I felt there was a larger sounding bull there with him. We soon found out I was right, as a much larger bull came out of the woods and was now standing in the marsh grass looking at the other bull.

I offered the big bull to Dale, but he said, "No, you shoot him," so at the count of three we both shot. My bull staggered and started to run, so I shot him again and he fell in the grass with a big splash. Dale emptied his gun at the smaller bull and in his excitement of seeing such a large animal so close, he never even touched him. I offered Dale my gun but he refused, so I shot the bull in the neck and he dropped like a rock right where he stood.

I don't think the young bull had ever heard a gunshot before, and we were hiding in the tall marsh grass so he probably was wondering what all the noise was about. All we could see of my moose now was a tip of one antler. We checked out Dale's moose and then went over across the creek to where mine lay. He was a dandy with a 51-inch spread, and Dale's had a 42-inch spread.

It was a perfect place to dress out the two moose. Dale's was high and dry on the point, and mine was in about six inches of water. This is the time that the work begins, but I personally enjoy every part of it. Dale, being a farm boy, was familiar with how to dress out an animal but never in these conditions. We took care of both moose then headed back to our tent camp to celebrate. The next day all four of us cut up the animals and hauled them back to camp. Four moose and four men was a lot to fly out of the bush. It took three trips with the Beaver, but that is all part of the great sport of moose hunting.

Again the following year, Dick, Charlie, my buddy Frank Tozser and I flew into Bragh Lake with Lee Cole's Flying Service. It was a beautiful day for flying and we had a very nice cabin which was a luxury for us. The lake was long and narrow, but there were two other parties that had been flown in by another outfitter. This kind of started our hunt out on a sour note, but we made the best of it and prepared for our hunt the following morning.

We hunted hard for four days and no moose. Our groceries were running low as we figured on some moose meat for a few meals. All of us were in camp one noon for sandwiches, dreaming of a good steak. There was a large window in the front of our cabin overlooking the lake and we were resting and enjoying the view, when a small black bear ran across the front yard.

We all jumped for our guns, but I got to the door first and got a shot into the bear. Just as he disappeared among some blown down trees I could see the bear and was about to shoot it again when Dick said, “Don't shoot it again, you'll spoil a lot of meat!” Dick grabbed a good sized club and climbed on top of the logs right over the bear, who in the confusion lifted his head up. Dick whacked him with the club several times until finally the bear was dead.

Like a bunch of hungry savages we gutted and skinned the bear, then quartered it and hung it on the meat pole. We also gave a quarter to the other hunters who had come down to see what all of the noise was about.

Dick cooked a dandy meal of bear steaks, and we ate the rest of the bear over the next day or two. Then the plane came and took us back to the base camp—empty handed. I believe this was our first time moose hunting that we got skunked. But we had a week of communing with nature in God's Country and lot of good companionship.

Hank's Moose

The following season we flew with George Theriolt out of Chapleau, Ontario. Our party was Dick, Charlie, Hank Johnson and I. Hank was from Royal Oak, Michigan and he was my hunting partner that year. Moose hunting is a lot of hard work and you have to be a little crazy and part sadist to enjoy it. Dick, Charlie, and I loved every minute of it. Hank was all pumped up after hearing about our previous hunts and I called him every day for 10 days before the hunt, egging him on.

We had a pretty decent cabin on an island, and after settling in we decided to check out the area and familiarize ourselves with the lake and surrounding marshes and rivers. We had flown into camp through snow squalls and it was quite cold, so we dressed accordingly. Dick and Charlie went southeast to check out a big marsh, and Hank and I decided to check out a river that flowed into our lake from the southwest.

There was quite a bit of moose sign, but after going up river maybe three miles we started to drift back with the current. There was a pretty stiff wind blowing, however we had a good current and I was able to navigate real well using an oar for a rudder. About a mile from the lake we rounded a curve and there stood a real nice bull moose, munching on some lily pad roots! We were only about 50 yards from the moose so I told Hank to shoot it, but only in the lung area so it would go to the shore and then he could drop it with a neck shot.

His response was, "My gun is not loaded!" I handed him my gun, as I really wanted him to kill the moose—and would you believe it—Hank shot the darn thing in the neck and killed it right in about three feet of water!

"What do we do now?" he asked, as he looked at the big animal lying in the water. My reply was, "Jump right in and get to work!"

The air was cold and so was the water, but we had to take care of our moose. We pulled him as close to shore as we could, then attached nylon ropes through his hamstrings, and at least got him turned on his back with his legs tied to two trees. We were then able to gut him out.

It was too late to go back for our block and tackle, so we left the moose half-in and half-out of the water. We were completely soaked and had about two miles of open lake to cross. It was getting real windy, much colder, and now there were snow showers. Hank was sitting in the front of the boat and shivering like crazy. I got my pack out as I always carry a little six-ounce flask of good old Seagrams 83 whiskey to toast our moose when we shoot them. Hank very seldom drank anything like that, but after I took a swig to our moose I handed him the flask and never did get it back until we got back to camp—empty! To this day he claims that saved his life. We never even got the sniffles from our cold, wet experience.

Dick and Charlie had also shot a bull at the edge of a marsh—nice and high and dry. The next morning all four of us armed with block and tackle, waders, and good sharp knives, went back to Hank's moose to cut it up and bring it back to camp. After a good meal we went and did the same thing to the other bull, and by nightfall we were all pooped but happy.

We decided we had enough meat so we spent the next few days fishing, relaxing, and partridge hunting. We always carried slingshots and marbles to shoot lots of spruce hens and partridge this way. The birds would run ahead of you or sit in the pine trees and would let you get real close. I tried several times to kill them by throwing a knife at them, but never did kill one that way.

This was Hank's first and last moose hunt. There is a lot of work involved and you have to be a special breed of cat to go and enjoy every facet of moose hunting. Gosh, I enjoy every bit of it and treasure all the memories of my many hunts.

Flying & Nushatogaini Lake

Over the years my sport shop had grown from a few cards of crawler harnesses and miscellaneous fishing supplies displayed in the hallway of mum and dad's house, to a shed in the back of their house. I added on to the shed, bought some metal horse troughs and really went into selling minnows.

This continued to grow and I got the chance to buy a piece of property on the highway. It was right across from our resort, and consisted of 100x600 feet of land with a small house on it, and a 18x24 foot building which I converted into a sport shop.

We all pitched in to help—mum, dad, Edythe, Donna Kay, and Butch small as he was, helped too. We added space each year and rented boats and motors. We used a spare lot on the lake that was part of our resort property where we kept our dock and boats. The place continued to grow and we added big storage barns for our customer's boats as well.

Our first mechanic was Ron Dickerson who stayed with us 30 years. He owned a share in an old Piper Cub airplane and a camp permit from Ontario, Canada for a fly-in camp. He kept bugging me to take up flying and buy into their plane and camp so much, that I finally agreed to fly up with him and look the situation over.

I really was not keen on flying, as I had several experiences in the South Pacific involving both friendly and unfriendly aircraft. But the lure of fishing and getting away from the rat race lured me into agreeing to go to Canada with him. The day arrived and we packed our gear and groceries into the little Cub which was quite a squeeze. After hand propping the engine we took off from our lake and headed north to Canada.

We had to land in the river at Sault Ste. Marie, Ontario for customs to come out and clear us to go into the bush. Having no radio in the plane, we had to telephone customs and sit on the dock until they came out and checked our gear and issued us a permit to fly into bush country. This was really an experience, and with no navigational aids we flew over lakes, mountains, and streams to our destination which was a very remote lake called Nushatogaini—which was named by native Cree Indians and means "Good Waters". It was, and still is, the closest place to Heaven in this world.

The lake is about 3-1/2 miles long and about 1/4 mile wide and about 20 miles from the closest road. The camp consisted of an old squad tent, two old canoes, a three burner gas stove, lantern, pots and pans, and four army cots. To our surprise there were four complete strangers with an old wooden boat using Ron's camp when we arrived. Some outfitter had flown them in and was commercializing on Ron's camp, which was strictly illegal.

The poor guys felt terrible as they had been told it belonged to the flying service. We made the best of it and Ron and I spent the night on the floor. It rained all night and we got wet and did not get much sleep. The next morning the plane came in to pick up the four men and we chewed the pilot out from stem to stern. We told him we were going to turn him in to the police, sink his boat, and if he ever showed up on the lake again that we would shoot holes in his plane's pontoons. After they left we chopped holes in the boat, filled it with rocks and sank it in 80 feet of water. To this day the pilot has never come back.

Ron and his other partners needed a couple more partners to improve their operation. I was sold, but only on the promise that we would build a cabin. We searched the lake for a good site and found a nice spot that formed a point into the lake. By opening a small channel next to the mainland we created an island.

On the way home Ron let me fly the J-3 Cub and I was really hooked on flying. None of us had much money, but we had a dream of what could be done.

We began a project of scrounging everything we could to completely equip a cabin. A gas and wood cook stove, gas refrigerator, tables, chairs, dishes, pots and pans, blankets, and what have you—including a boat and motor that were donated by friends and relatives. We loaded a truck full of supplies and equipment, then headed for Chapleau, Ontario where we had arranged to have a big old Norseman aircraft fly in our goodies, plus timber to frame in our cabin. The best account is a copy of the events as reported by our local paper:

OTSEGO COUNTY HERALD-TIMES,
GAYLORD, MICHIGAN
THURSDAY, SEPTEMBER 9, 1966

AREA IS CLEARED AND DOCKS BUILT:
CABIN IS BUILT IN THREE DAYS....IN SPITE OF RAIN

Shades of Daniel Boone and Davey Crockett, with the modern versions substitution cameras and sea-planes for rifles and a horse. Two hundred air miles north and a trifle east of Gaylord lies Nushatogaini Lake. In the lake there is a two acre island, and on that island now stands a very complete cabin which wasn't there just a week ago. Thereby hangs this tale.

On Friday evening, August 20, Ron Dickerson and his son, Dennis, Louie Brandenburg, Cleo Hoxie and Jerry Glasser set out, by truck, for this remote spot for which the men have a use-permit. On the truck (among other things) were mattresses, a stove and refrigerator, a portable light plant, all kinds of tools, doors and windows, weather-proofing material, pots and pans, food,—you name it, and they had it. By comparison, "Ma" Clampett is a piker!

This group of self-styled gypsies drove as far as the spot called Flame Lake. There they were met by Sandy Storing and Dick Shields who had flown up to the lake. All day Saturday there was action, The Thunder Mountain Shuttle Service. Trip after trip was made, to fly all the stuff from the truck stop to the island. It took all day.

On Saturday, August 21, Don Butcher and Emil Kaspala drove as far as the Soo, where Bob Nichols met them and they all flew to this island hide-a-way.

Bob had been with another group of men who were fishing even farther north than Nushatogaini Lake. (Are you still with us?) By bed-time Saturday night, the floor of the 16 by 20 cabin plus an 8 foot porch, was finished and level, and ready for the mattresses and sleeping bags.

It was a balmy and clear night, but just to be safe, the intrepid woodsmen stretched a plastic tarp of sorts, for protection. By 1 AM the rain came, in spades! It rained all night. The plastic tarp cracked and collapsed. Everyone and everything was thoroughly soaked. The Boones and the Crocketts began to have some second thoughts.

The rains continued all day Sunday, but by that evening, all four cabin walls were up, the roof was on, and the cabin had been weather proofed. Of course the area had to be cleared of brush and trees before any of this could happen.

Two docks were built, one to use for fishing and swimming, and one large enough for the docking of three seaplanes. The island is separated from the mainland by a beaver channel, so the men had to build a bridge. If the moose and fish don't cooperate after all of this -- there ought to be a law.

A boat and a canoe which had also been on that truck, were taken to Chapleau and flown to the island on a big Norseman plane. According to Don Butcher, the cabin is now almost ready for the inspection by the wives. Built are two sets of double-bunk beds, drawer space and a small dressing room. The oil heating unit is all ready to go, and the ladies may have their choice of cooking on either a gas or wood stove. To round out the modern facilities is a big gas refrigerator. Butcher says that everything they have has been either begged, borrowed or stolen!

The members of the Thunder Mountain Flying Club, (who own the plane) are Sandy Storing, Ron Dickerson, Kermit Brink and Don Butcher. Add the names of Dick Shields and Emil Kaspala and you have the six members of the Nushatogaini Lake Club.

Three of the men left for home on Monday, August 23, with Butcher, Dickerson and Brandenburg due to fly home on Tuesday. To make this safari experience complete, the trio was completely fogbound on Tuesday. They spent the time clearing more ground and flew safely home on Wednesday.

•••

During our work bee framing in our cabin, Ron, Sandy, and I flew three planes over to an old abandoned lumber camp where we tore down an old building and took the lumber which we tied onto our pontoons and headed back to our island. We made many trips flying lumber and bricks from an old kiln which we used for many jobs. The lumber was used to build an outhouse on the mainland as we wanted NO S--T on our island!

We built a walking bridge across the channel we had made to make our point of land an island, and it has worked just great for the last 30 plus years. We also built a boat house to keep our motors, gas cans and the like, in out of the weather when we were not there. The lumber we got for nothing also made us our first dock.

All of this took place over a year or so while I had the privilege of learning to fly with the best instructor that ever lived, Bob Nichols. He knew that I wanted to be a bush pilot and he taught me all kinds of things that were not in the book. Bob put me through all kinds of maneuvers and showed how to cope with them.

He once sent me down to Houghton Lake while the plane was on skis, and he asked me to pick up five gallons of gas. I questioned whether there would be snow to land on, and he said of course there was. You guessed it—when I got there, there wasn't any snow on the runways. However, on the side of the runways between the tufts of grass was a little snow, so I came in and then touched down on the grass. The airport manager signed my student book for a cross country flight, then sold me the gas. He then helped me turn the plane around, propped the plane, and I was off.

Just a few miles north I flew into one heck of a snowstorm and quickly found out that you could not see anything straight ahead. I could see the ground though, so I flew west until I could see the highway which I followed to the north end of Bradford Lake. I made an about right turn and there was the airport as I had figured, and there was Nichols with a big smile on his face.

After much studying and book work, I passed my exams and was given my license to fly any single engine plane—land or sea type. Over the next 30-plus years and over 1,800 hours as P.I.C. (Pilot In Command), we flew many, many trips to our cabin in Canada and lots of other places.

My first trip to Beaver Island, which lays about 20

miles out in Lake Michigan, was a real interesting trip. My instructor Nichols and I plotted our direction, time, and distance over many checkpoints and away we went. It was a beautiful day and everything was going really well until we hit our check point—Harbor Springs, which sits northwest of Petoskey and right on the shore of Lake Michigan—when we ran into a big fog bank (I really believe Nichols knew this before we left).

He said, "Lets go to our destination," which was about 15 miles straight west of our location. I had flown with Bob under the hood and in the clouds before, but never in fog. We bore ahead at 2,000 feet altitude strictly on instruments. I had checked my time and knew when we should arrive at Beaver Island if I flew our air speed at 85 miles-per-hour and kept our altitude.

It was quite an unnerving experience and I was really sweating. Bob was no help either, trying to tell me we had passed the island and turn back—but my time and instruments said otherwise. When the time was up we descended through the fog and haze and lo and behold there was the island. Boy, what a relief! We landed at St. James Bay and had lunch. By that time the fog had cleared enough that we could see the mainland, and we had a safe, uneventful flight home.

Two of the worst places to fly are through the Straits of Mackinac and through the Sault Ste. Marie area. Both of these areas are between two of the Great Lakes and have a lot of fog, wind, and rain while other areas just a few miles north or south are blessed with real good weather.

I remember one trip to Canada with my son Butch. We had great weather up to the Straits of Mackinac, and then ran into a solid fog bank. We landed at Mackinac and taxied up to the shore where we tied up our plane and proceeded to wait until the fog lifted—which it usually does, but not this day. We slept on the beach that night and come morning, lo and behold, the fog was still there. We waited a couple of hours, then I called the airport at St. Ignace which was about 10 miles north. He informed me that the weather was beautiful there, so he advised me to climb to about 3,000 feet and we should clear the fog.

Off we went, and such a beautiful sight. He was 100 percent right, at 3,000 feet it was as clear as a bell and we could see for miles. We did not know it at the time, but my mechanic Ron was sitting at St. Ignace with his plane waiting to come home to Gaylord. When he saw us fly over he knew it must be OK to the south, so he flew over the fog and went home. They say for small planes of our type—If you have time to spare...fly by air.

We had only a minimum of instruments, so all of our flying was done by VFR—Visual Flight Rules, or Pilotage—knowing and seeing where you were going. Basically, it was flying by the seat of your pants. Once we cleared customs at Sault Ste. Marie there were no navigation aids or help. You flew strictly by the maps, and you had to keep on your toes or you could get lost very easily. Over the years we had to land in many different lakes due to bad weather we would encounter. We made quite a few friends this way and everyone would bend over backwards to help out.

Above: Our island on Nushatogaini Lake, taken through the wing struts of our plane.

Below: An inside view of our cabin today. Rough living for a cabin in bush country.

Gene And My First Plane Crash

Gene Williams, a former partner in my Piper Super Cruiser, made a lot of money in the oil and gas business and had bought a Cessna 180. He had recently qualified for an IFR rating, so he could fly strictly by instruments in adverse weather. To keep your rating, you had to fly so many hours to stay current.

One day he stopped at the office and asked if I would fly with him as an observer to Pellston, Michigan and back to Gaylord. After checking the weather and his airplane we taxied out on the runway and got clearance to take off. He put the hood on his head, and away we went. It was a real nice day for flying and we arrived at Pellston, landed and had a cup of coffee, then took off for the return trip to Gaylord. Gene removed his hood, and as the wind changed he decided to land on the north/

south runway which was not paved. It was strictly a sod strip. I believe he was thinking he was flying on floats because he did not have a good angle on his approach. Immediately on touch down the plane flipped over on its back, and the tail plowed a deep furrow in the grass strip.

Gene was lying all in a heap behind me as his safety belt had broken, and I was hanging upside down in mine. After pulling myself up a little I was able to unhook my safety belt and drop down to the ceiling of the plane, which being upside down was now like the floor. I could smell gas, so I made sure the switches were off and hauled Gene out of the plane. He was bleeding pretty bad from a cut on his forehead, but was able to hobble along with my help to get away from the plane in case it caught fire.

It was early evening so we were not able to notify the tower that we were coming in for a landing, and evidently no one had seen us come in. We sat there and got his cut to stop bleeding.

"Look at my plane!" he said. "Just think of what it's going to cost to fix it." That is when I told him, "Just be damned glad we were both able to walk away and not get killed."

After sitting there for a while longer, we walked to the terminal which was about three-fourths of a mile and called our wives. We then called the FAA and the police to properly report the accident, and were both taken to the hospital.

Gene had a broken sternum and a few cuts, and had to stay in the hospital a couple of days. I had a lot of bruises and some severe contusions from my waist down to my knees and was released to go home. My body turned black and blue for about three weeks, and then returned back to normal.

Gene had his plane repaired and then sold it. He has not bought another one yet. Just a few days after the accident I climbed into my float plane and flew for about an hour all by myself, just to make sure the trauma of the accident would not affect my desire to fly. Thank the good Lord I flew again for many years.

Nushatogaini Bears

The first incident we had with bears was a disaster. We had flown up with three planes to do some finishing work on our cabin, and upon arrival we found our door all smashed in as were the porch windows. We had earlier flown in three bags of mortar to make an outdoor barbecue, and the darn bears had really made a mess of the place.

They took canned goods, crunched them in and sucked out the contents. They chewed on the handle of our pride and joy—namely our gas refrigerator—until the door opened, then stuck their paws into the controls, mangling them so that the fridge was useless. Naturally they ate everything, including a lot of eggs mixed with mortar and bear poop. They tore up our bunk beds and our blankets in that awful mess. The darn bears even chewed up some of our pots and pans, putting teeth marks the size of a rifle bullet through the metal which completely ruined them.

The place was a complete shambles, so we cut a hole in the floor and formed a bucket brigade hauling water from the lake and throwing it on the walls, ceiling, and floor. Then we broomed it all outside. Everything in the cabin had to be washed in the lake before we could use it again.

I was so mad I flew into Chapleau about 40 miles north of our camp and went to the head man of the Game Division of the Lands and Forest. I lodged a very loud and angry complaint against the bear damage to our cabin. Mr. McVeigh was his name, and he took me into his office and informed me that they were the Queen's bears and that nothing could be done about it!

I politely informed him that from now on any bears we saw around our island, we were going to kill them whether they were giants or cubs. He walked over and closed the door to his office and in a hushed voice said, "Mr. Butcher, will you do me a favor? If you kill the bloody bears, kindly get rid of the carcasses!"

So the war with the bears was on.

We repaired our door and windows, made shutters for the windows and built a real sturdy plank door to cover our regular door. We were sure our cabin was bear proof now! How wrong we were!

My wife, Edythe, and I went up for a week's vacation shortly after our bear episode, and I could see signs on our island that a bear had been there quite recently. That night I laid our old 12 gauge pump shotgun on the table loaded with slugs, and next to it was a six-volt lantern. Edythe wanted to know what I was doing and I told her it was just a precaution in case any animals came around.

It was a beautiful moonlit night, very calm and quiet. I was awakened about 11 PM by the noise of something moving and rubbing on the cabin right next to where I was lying. Then, all of a sudden, a big black bear stood up and started to push on our front door! I grabbed the shotgun and was going to shoot him silhouetted against the door, but my plane was tied to the dock right behind him. I opened our inside door which was only eight feet from where he stood, and hollered at the bear who dropped down on all fours and disappeared.

I waited a couple of minutes then opened the outside door, but could not see or hear him. All of a sudden he stood up on his back legs and started to growl and pop his teeth. Man, he looked 10 feet tall and three feet wide to me. Being black, it was hard to pick a spot on him, so I aimed at the sky and brought the barrel down until it disappeared in the black and pulled the trigger. Boy, it sounded like a cannon going off and the sound echoed off the high rock walls of the lake two or three times. Then all was quiet.

Edythe jumped out of bed and said, "Did you get him?" My reply was, "I don't know, it's all quiet out there. Bring the flashlight and shine it by the corner of the cabin."

She was so excited she shined the light in the trees, on my plane and everywhere but where I wanted it. I took the flashlight and lo and behold there laid the bear flat on the ground, just like it was sleeping. What a lucky shot! I had hit him square in the forehead and he died instantly. The next morning when I went to pull him down the hill into the boat to dispose of the carcass in a rock gorge, I noticed the slug had gone right through the bear and had put a hole in one of the canoes that was hanging on a rack right behind him.

We have since taken old boards and driven nails through them and placed them, nails up, under each window and on our steps. We call these our bear welcome mats!

Everything went well until the next fall when our son Butch and I took our annual father/son vacation when we usually winterize the camp. The first thing upon our arrival we always check for bear damage. Everything looked fine until we got to the west side of the cabin. That darn bear must have smelled some of our goodies in a wall cupboard that was situated between two windows.

He tore off the plywood siding, cuffed out the insulation then punched the inside plywood into the cabin. He then entered through the hole in the wall. We must have scared the bear away because there were fresh muddy tracks on the floor when we opened the cabin. Right then war was declared and I told Butch we were going to get that rascal that night.

I took some old tin cans and tied them between two trees and also ran a few cans down to the ground where we put some chicken bones and skin that we had eaten for lunch. I got the shotgun out and put in three slugs, and got the flashlight out and laid them all on the table for when the bear would come.

Butch could not believe that I was so confident we would get him, but he did not know what I had in mind to coax him to our food bait. Butch wanted me to be the one to shoot the bear, so his job was to put the light on the critter when he moved some of our cans. I built a real hot fire in our wood stove, then poured honey on the hot coals and we went to bed.

About 10 PM we heard the cans tinkle and both of us jumped up. I grabbed the gun and Butch took the light, and when I was ready to shoot Butch flipped the light on. The bear looked up and looked like he had been caught with his paw in the cookie jar. That was his last thought, and when I shot he dropped right on the chicken bones.

Butch was really excited and when he saw the bear twitch a little he said, “Shoot him again, dad.” So this time I shot him in the head. The next morning we took the bear to the same spot where I disposed of the first bear. When we got back we found that one of the slugs had gone through the bear and ricochetted off the rocks and put another hole in a canoe on the rack behind the bear.

After this episode we made more bear pads and strung them on the ground all around the cabin, and so far we have not been bothered again.

I forgot to mention that one year I had buried about a dozen cans of beer in a hole below some pine trees to hide them from my hunting buddies and a darn bear must have smelled either me or the beer, because he dug them up and bit every can in the middle and sucked out the beer! He must have been one happy bear for a while. Needless to say, bears and Gray Wolf don't mix too well.

Nushatogaini and Shorty

My wife, Edythe, and I have many fond memories of vacationing at our island in Canada. We would pack all our goodies into our seaplane that we kept at Otsego Lake where our home is, and fly off to Sault Ste. Marie, Ontario. There we had to land and be checked out by the Canadian customs, gas the plane and then set off cross country to our beloved island at Nushatogaini Lake.

This is beautiful country to fly over with mountains and hundreds of lakes in all shapes and sizes. Without navigational aides, you learn to believe your maps and compass or you can get hopelessly lost. We thoroughly enjoy this wilderness. The loons, seagulls, and ospreys, as well as mink, otter, and moose all make it a paradise away from home. We often take a boat to the south end of our lake, then take a short portage across to what we

Above: My wife and fishing partner Edythe, showing off a nice Nusha' pike on our front dock. Our cabin and guests are in the background.

Below: Edythe and I with our granddaughter Wendy holding up a few tasty walleye.

simply call Lake Number One. Here, we leave two or three canoes year-round for us and our friends to use. We use side motor mounts and 4hp Evinrude outboards to traverse those waters.

From here, there are a series of four small lakes connected by streams followed by a rapids that we have to pull or carry our gear over. After the rapids there are four more "chain lakes" which eventually lead to a second rapids. It is a beautiful trip with good fishing for northern pike, walleye, and both lake and brook trout. We pack a lunch that we eat at different spots and spend the whole day in canoes.

Several times while I would be landing a fish, Edythe would reel her line in and just for something to do she would splash her lure just in front of the canoe. I surely wish I had a video of this, because out of nowhere a fish would tug the line down and she would pull it back up just hollering and screaming for help! Believe it or not, several good fish have gone on our stringer by this method.

It was not uncommon to catch 10 to 20-pound fish "down river" as we called it. I remember one instance that I hooked onto a lunker pike, and I had a real battle with it. Upon tiring it out I attempted to net it, but it was so big I could only get its head and part of its body into the net. I put down my rod, grabbed the net with both hands and heaved this monster into the canoe.

Boy, holy hell broke loose then. The pike was thrashing around in the bottom of the canoe, throwing tackle boxes and gear all over the place and Edythe was screaming her head off. I straddled the pike with my knees and legs, grabbed a bottle of Coca-Cola and rapped him soundly in the head a couple of times. I was not about to trust a regular stringer, and used a piece of nylon rope to tie it up.

At 44-1/2 inches long and weighing 34-3/4 pounds this was, and still is, our camp record. This had to be some kind of record, but we brought it home and gave it to a friend who ate it at a family gathering they had.

Edythe and I have spent many days all by ourselves on our beautiful river system. One day it was quite windy and we were in the second lake when a cow moose and two calves came out and fed in a small marsh really close to us. Then an osprey flew over and all of a sudden he dove right under the water and came up with a fish in his talons. He tried to fly out of the lake area, but with his load of fish he could not get enough altitude to clear the trees. After flying around the lake a couple of times he flew off, probably to feed his babies.

We have watched the loons do their mating dance, and carry their babies on their backs, and have spent lots of time watching the beavers go about their chores. On different occasions we have boated right up to the beaver houses and listened to the baby beavers mewing inside of their lodges.

We are so fortunate for being able to enjoy nature at its very best at our Shangri-la in Canada. We have enjoyed our camp for over 30 years. But sadly, age is making our trips harder every year. I am now 81 years young and Edythe turned 85 this September.

Edythe and I with my bread wrapper hat on our front dock, ready for another peaceful day of fishing.

Gertrude and Heathcliff

We have a pair of seagulls that each year come back to our island and they have their nest on a big rock that is about 50 yards from the shore. I am sure they picked this spot to keep animals from getting to their eggs and young chicks.

These gulls have become quite tame, almost to hand feed them. We named them Gertrude and Heathcliff—names from the Red Skelton show. Heathcliff is the largest gull I have ever seen, and has a crest on his head like an eagle. For many years they have returned to our beloved island. We feed them all of our table scraps and fish guts that we put on a rock about 20 feet out in the lake.

We built a split-log walkway from the island out to the rock, and thoroughly enjoy watching and talking to these birds. When we start our motors to go fishing I will give them a whistle, and pretty soon here they come following our boat and looking for handouts. They will follow us all day even if we go down river, and they will follow us back home at night.

Several years ago I had a strange experience. This was late in the fall and Heathcliff came to our rock with one of their babies. I swear that he was trying to tell me that this was probably his last trip, and he was introducing me to his son, and at the same time letting the young gull know that I was OK to be around. The following year Heathcliff did not return, but his son did—along with his mate, and we now are enjoying their company each summer.

You might think I am crazy to believe such a thing, but it happened just as I told you. Animals and birds are very intelligent. How can these "uneducated" birds fly thousands of miles each year and return to the same remote lake without radar or compass? Could you accomplish such a feat? This is a God given gift and is truly amazing. I sincerely believe that after communing with nature, the birds, and the animals, that it would be impossible to be a heathen!

Grandkids At Nushatogaini

Al Beaulieu, commonly known as Smoky, is one of my best friends. Our two grandsons, Brian and Jeff, who have made several trips to our island in Canada, know him as Uncle Smoky. He has watched them grow up through the years and is almost like a nanny to them. Between our trips to Canada and deer hunting at our Eight Ball property, he has been with us. We have both given the boys a good knowledge of how to appreciate the outdoors and how to be good sportsmen in all their activities.

In our trips up to our Shangri-la I would fly-in one of our grandsons, while Smoky would drive Edythe and our other grandson up in my Suburban. On the return trip I would swap grandsons and fly the other one home. After opening the cabin and boathouse we usually had a lunch then cut the cards to see who would fish with whom that day. We always had a 10-cent bet on for the largest fish to create some excitement, which it usually did. We catch walleye, pike and lake trout and eat like kings. We have steak, chicken and lots of fish with all the trimmings. Smoky is a real good cook, which makes the trips more enjoyable for my wife.

I remember one day Jeff was with grandma and I, and it was quite windy. We had caught some nice eating size walleyes for our supper and noticed that Brian and Smoky were in real close to the weeds near shore. We could see Brian pick up the landing net quite often, so we motored across the lake to see what they were up to. When we arrived we found that Brian had tossed out the anchor before looking to see if it was tied to the boat—well, you guessed it, it wasn't. He had been trying to either snag the rope or the anchor with the landing net, but the wind was blowing them around too much. We went back to camp and returned the next morning while it was calm and found it quite easily.

Another day, Brian was fishing with Edythe and I, and we came across a nice, big cow moose feeding on the lily pads at the mouth of a little stream we call Brandenburg Creek. We went over to where Jeff and Smoky were fishing and told them where the moose was. They went over to watch the cow, but Jeff was saying, "keep going closer," until the old cow had enough and climbed out of the water—going into the woods to get away from the nosy intruders.

One day the boys had an idea and gathered a bush saw, axe, hammer and spikes along with a long, half-inch braided nylon rope and headed across our little bridge to the mainland. They made their way to a cliff-like rock with a sheer face that dropped straight into the lake where it was about 20 feet deep. They cut a cross-brace, spiked it onto two solid birch trees and tied the rope to the cross arm. Grabbing the rope, they would back up a few paces and swing out over the water before letting go and dropping into the lake. This project provided them a chance to work off a lot of energy and many hours of just plain old fun.

One trip, we were having trouble getting the right kind of shiner minnows to use for pike fishing. I knew of a lake where there were plenty of that type of minnow, but it meant a trip down river to get them. So we packed a lunch and a couple of minnow traps, tossed in our fishing gear and away we went. We have two canoes stashed in the bush across from the portage, so it was real easy to take our gear across and load them up to head down river.

Our destination was a little lake that sat atop a big hill behind the third lake in our river system. We call this Bean Lake because it looks like a bean when you fly over it. There is a nice path from the main river up the hill to the lake, but in places it is quite steep. Upon arriving at the lake, we climbed into the canoe we leave there for fishing and also for moose hunting. We set our traps and caught a few big shiners by hook and line as well.

When we left to go back to the river we could not take all the minnows we caught in the traps, so we dumped a whole bucket of shiners back into the lake and proceeded to go down the trail. Jeff was carrying the two minnow buckets and tried to hurry up going down the steepest part of the trail. Well, he tripped and went head over heels with the buckets—and consequently we lost 90 percent of the bait. Oh well, that's the way things happen!

We decided to troll for walleyes on the way home and Jeff and I had a nice stringer of them between two and three pounds each. We had visions of a good fish supper but that's not what we got that night. When we went to pull up our stringer, it was gone! We will never know what happened—whether there was a weak link in the stringer, or maybe a big pike might have nailed one of the fish and pulled the stringer loose.

We have lost fish off our stringers that we have tied to the dock until we are ready to clean them. In fact, twice we have lifted a stringer of walleyes from our dock only to find a huge pike with a walleye half way down his throat! Both times we have grabbed the pike and ended up with a real nice trophy without even fishing for them!

We have had many picnics at the north end of the lake because there is a beautiful sand beach there and it goes from about a foot deep at the shore to eight to ten feet pretty quick. The kids like to run and jump into the lake and swim there close to shore. Most of our shoreline is very rocky so this is a real treat for the boys. There are always moose and bear tracks in the sand, which are always a big thrill to observe. There is never a dull moment at our camp at Nushatogaini, and we are very grateful to have enjoyed our children and grandchildren at such a heavenly spot.

NUSHATOGAINI MEMBERS

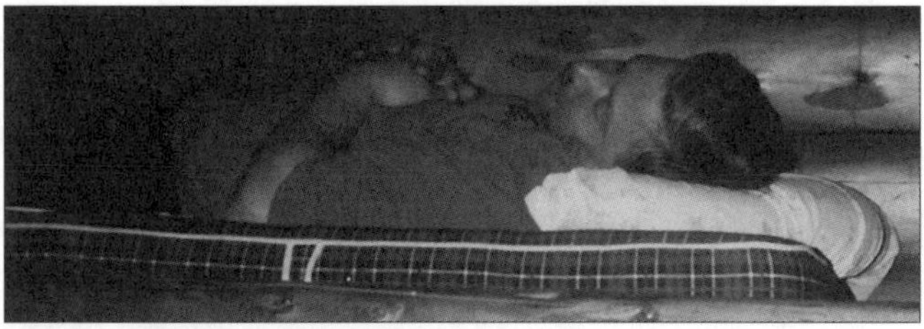

Bob Caras—holding down the fort.

A toast with Dick Shiels.

Ron Dickerson and Gray Wolf.

Emil Kaspala with two Canadian moose hunters.

MORE OF CANADA

Above: Bob Hancock and Gray Wolf with my Super Cruiser "Betsy".

Left: Bob King with a nice catch of fresh Nushatogaini Pike.

Below: One way in, one way out, (unless you walk out, which I personally don't recommend).

Start Of The Eight Ball Club

There were eight of us who had hunted together for about 20 years and we decided we would like to own our own hunting camp, so being in the real estate business I started looking for property. After much research I found a place about 23 miles north and east of Otsego Lake that really appealed to all of us.

It consisted of 139 acres of quite heavily timbered land with two small fields on it. The owners wanted to keep their old cabin and about 12 acres, so we planned on putting a trailer on what we were going to buy. We made an offer and they accepted, and we bought it on a land contract. That summer one of the owners of the cabin died and the other two wanted to sell it, so we bought the cabin and the 12 acres that adjoined our land.

The cabin was a real dingy old place that had been neglected but was structurally sound. It had a real nice fieldstone fireplace, a big living and dining area, a front porch, and two bedrooms. After several "work bees" we had it all cleaned up and moved the kitchen from the living room into the front porch. We also put in a nice sink and cupboards that we scrounged from somewhere. We were in good shape for the upcoming deer season and had a great time in our own camp. We named it the Eight Ball Club and we set up a set of rules and regulations as to its operation and usage.

The first deer season, Jerry Johnson invited his wife along and that just did not work out at all, so we talked it over and voted him out of the club and bought out his share. We had our wives sign off their dower rights to the property, and to protect our friendships and future troubles made it part of our bylaws that no women be allowed to hunt during the deer season. We had all known one another for many years and had hunted together for as many also, and wanted a place to relax and enjoy one another's company for years to come.

The first year we drew a blank, never shot a buck, but had great plans for the next year. We had two work bees a year, one in May and one in October so we could all get together to work on the camp and property. A good friend of mine, Ralph Pichan, taught me how to run a bulldozer and left his machine there for us to use to clean up and make roads to get better access to our hunting spots. We really put in a great system of trails that have worked out very well for us. We also built blinds so it would be more comfortable for us to hunt from.

Over the years we have painted the cabin, built on a modern bathroom—complete with a shower and hot water—built a storage shed and also a real nice sauna steam building. We really rough it with all the comforts of home.

We are now a registered tree farm and manage our property with a clear cut and several select timber cuts to enhance it for deer hunting and proper management of our woods. The clear cut has now regrown into a real nice thick cover and we have even built a small pond, lined with rubber so the wildlife has a place to drink.

The oil and gas industry hit our area and we have negotiated several deals with them for pipe lines and a gas storage for storing natural gas under our property. We really cut a deal on this storage field, making enough money to pay off our camp. Each man got a dividend and put money in the bank to pay for improving our camp and to buy some equipment to maintain our roads and fields.

Oh yes, we also had a 30x40 foot pole barn built to keep our equipment in. The latest project was building a large woodshed by the cabin as we do use the fireplace quite a bit. Our old fuel-oil stove was replaced with a new gas furnace and we squared off our building and are now in the process of finishing our second bathroom and storage room. We really have a nice lodge now and we use it a lot during the summer months for outings with our wives and friends.

We have lost three of our original members who passed away on to the Happy Hunting Grounds, but life must go on. Butch took over his father-in-law Hank Johnson's share. Brian Pelton took over his father Wayne Pelton's share. Terry Emerick took over Ray Pelton's share, who was his uncle. We now have seven members plus an honorary member, Smoky Beaulieu, who has and is working his butt off improving our camp and property.

One recent fall we planted 7,000 spruce and pine trees, plus many wildlife packets of shrubs to provide food and cover for our deer. We also now have six fields of buckwheat, alfalfa, clover, and rye. It is a lot of work but we love doing it, and are quite proud of our Shangri-la.

Of course, our deer have contributed to the camp by providing us with a considerable amount of venison, and quite a few wild turkeys have donated to our freezers. We have a good crop of raspberries, blackberries, and morel mushrooms, so you can see we do use and benefit from our land.

Each season our buck kill has varied from zero for seven to six for seven, depending on weather and other factors. Several years ago I was feeling real bad with a cold and stomach flu, and really should not have been out in the woods, but there are only 15 days of deer hunting and I hate to miss any of them.

I crawled out of bed, sick as a dog, got dressed, and my old buddy Arnie Pawlitz dropped me off at the Valley Road which is about three-fourths of a mile from camp. My blind was only about 40 yards up a small hill and I practically crawled from the road to my little open-air stand. After arranging my lunch and rain gear where they would not be in the way if I saw a buck, I settled down and enjoyed the fact that this was opening morning.

Shortly after daylight, a doe and two fawns walked by and never gave me as much as a glance. About 7:30 AM, out of nowhere stood a nice buck at maybe 30 yards broadside. Slowly I raised up my old buddy, the .300 Savage, settled it on the buck and at the crack of the gun he dropped in his tracks. Now what?

I really did not look forward to crawling out there and dressing him out, but it had to be done. As sick as I was this was quite a chore. Somehow I did it and crawled back to my blind to enjoy the rest of the day.

For the first few days of the season I never leave my blind from daylight to dark, and you would not believe how many deer I see with the other hunters getting restless and going in for lunch. About noon Arnie came on his way to noon lunch and he and Frank loaded the buck up and took it to camp to hang on our buck pole, as I was too sick to help.

Our son Butch loves to hunt, but to keep peace in the family he only hunts the first day. I gave him my Number Two Blind and he has shot several bucks from this stand. A few years ago Butch and his younger son Jeff were not seeing any deer, so they came over to visit me and I suggested that they try my Hill Blind which was about 300 yards from their spot.

Jeff was making all kinds of noise trying to get a fire started when a big doe appeared from a draw between two hills only about 40 yards from where they were sitting. Right behind her was a real nice buck with his neck swelled up and his nose right at her butt. They couldn't care less about who was around or how much noise they were making, so Butch promptly shot the buck. He dropped but tried to get up, so Butch shot him again and did not realize what a nice buck it was until they scrambled out to gut him out as quickly as possible. It was a nicely formed 8-pointer with a 17-1/2 inch inside spread. We had the head mounted in a sneak form and it hangs proudly in Butch's computer room at the Sport Shop.

When our older grandson, Brian, became old enough we built him a nice blind about halfway between his dad's blind and where I hunt. He got spoiled right away, as early on opening morning a 6-point walked right by him and just about dared him to shoot it. He made a really good, clean kill with his .308 that I bought for him.

Grandson Brian's first buck. A six pointer he shot in 1989.

Starting them out early. Grandsons Jeff (left) and Brian (right).

I have made it a point to buy all our kids a good rifle and they were all trained well on how to use their weapons with the safety on, and where to place their shots for clean kills. They were also taught how to properly dress all types of game, how to read signs in the woods, and how to read maps and a compass to be able to find their way out to wherever they want to go, and to find their way back home again. They all thoroughly love the Great Outdoors that God has provided for us, and how to enjoy and respect all phases of it. I am very pleased and proud to have had a part in this portion of their education.

Shortly after we acquired the Eight Ball property, 180 acres in total, we had the opportunity to buy two 40 acre parcels adjoining the club on our north boundary. There were rumors of a motorcycle club wanting this acreage because of the hilly terrain. The Eight Ball members said no, so our son-in-law Bob King and I bought it as an investment and to give us more land. We had to pay a premium price for that 80 acres, but today it is worth over twice what we paid for it. We call it Heather Wood.

Two years later another 80 acres became available, so Bob, Frank Tozser, Arnie Pawlitz and I purchased this land essentially squaring off the Eight Ball property. Now, jointly we own over 350 acres. We call this new acreage the Four Ball property. The terrain of our new acquisition is very hilly and backs up to a big private tract of land. We have placed a few blinds there, but due to the big hills not too many want to hunt it, though the four of us have killed several nice bucks on this tract. It reminds me of hunting out West in the foothills of the Rocky Mountains!

We usually go out to camp about once a week to check the roads and work on our fields. After recently planting several thousand pine trees we have lots of things to do, but we love just being out in the woods and really enjoy doing this kind of work! We had an old Ford N9 tractor that we used for a lot of jobs but it just was not big enough to do what we wanted, so we traded it for a Ford Model

2120—a four-wheel drive diesel, which is a real joy to operate! As we get older we try to get better equipment, making our chores much easier. We also have a five yard dump truck to help with road work.

We have our two work bees every year—one in the middle of May when we all get together and work on fences, and the cabin, and pick morel mushrooms. Again in October we get together to put up wood for our fireplace and get things ready for deer hunting. In the summer of 1998, we purchased a real heavy duty log splitter so our chore of putting up the wood is much easier.

We are very fortunate to have this little slice of heaven and every year we use it more and more for birthday parties, berry picking, or just a relaxing drive around our roads, looking for elk, deer, turkeys, and even the occasional bear. It is truly one of life's plus factors communing with all of God's creation.

Brian Pelton, the newest member of the Eight Ball Club.

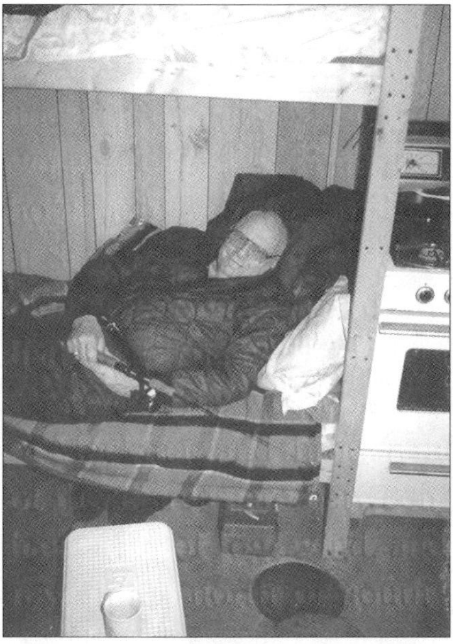

Solid comfort—fishing right through the floor!

Bungalow ice fishing 3-1/2 miles out on the lake!

EIGHT BALL CLUB

***Above:* Frank Tozser, Al "Smoky" Beaulieu and Gray Wolf in 1990.**

***Left:* At the Buck Pole. Frank, Gray Wolf and Paul Ruckle's son David.**

***Bottom left:* Betty Simmons, Paul Ruckle and my wife Edythe at camp.**

***Bottom right:* Bob Thomas, our newest hired man at the Eight Ball Club.**

****Deceased members:* Hank Johnson, Wayne Pelton, Ray Pelton.**

Above left: Terry Emerick at the Buck Pole.

Above right: Arnie Pawlitz, about to relax in front of a toasty fire at our camp.

Below: Father and Son. Butch and I in my office at the shop.

Eight Ball Turkeys

This title could be about any of our members, but real turkey hunting turned out to be a big plus for us. As a result of the DNR program to bring wild turkeys back to Michigan as a game bird, the implants took off like gang busters and before too long we had our first turkey hunt. It was a lottery type hunt. You paid a fee and the DNR held drawings for different areas and issued permits depending on the turkey count in each area. The first year Arnie, Frank, Smoky, Paul and I all drew permits. There were lots of birds and we each shot a nice gobbler. The meat is delicious and is very hard to tell from domesticated turkey if it is cooked properly.

Over the years we have been very lucky and also have learned each year how to call the wily old toms in. We use decoys and gobble, cluck and purr, each using the call we prefer. Frank was the first one to actually call in a tom turkey. He was sitting in Smoky's deer blind and almost shot the tom in self-defense, for it came running right up to his blind. He never knew what hit him as Frank scored with his old double barrel shot gun. He claims it was his super calling, but then there are other opinions including plain dumb luck!

My first tom turkey was also shot from one of our deer blinds. At the break of day I set out three decoys about 30 yards from the blind and sat back waiting for something to happen. Every once in a while I could hear a turkey gobble. Three deer walked by totally unaware of the fact that I was watching them. Just a short while later a tom gobbled to the southeast of me and I returned his call according to what I had read in magazines and from talking to other hunters at our Sport Shop.

The turkey and I talked to one another several times and it seemed to me that he was coming in from the east. Then he quit gobbling and I did likewise, all scooched down in my blind hoping and waiting. Not too long after this, out of the corner of my eye I caught a movement. I turned my head real slow and lo and behold that sly old tom circled around and sneaked in from the north. He was about 10 yards from me and all his attention was on my three decoys. I let him get out about 20 yards from me when my number 6 copper-coated shot ended his life quickly, sending him off to turkey heaven.

I was admiring my turkey when BOOM, another blast shook the woods. Smoky was hunting about 200 yards to the south of my blind and he had just talked another tom out of a small swale. With a well placed shot he ended another turkey's career. Smoky, Frank, Bob and I drew permits this spring (2001), but due to the scarcity of birds we all agreed to pass and hope for a good nesting season.

Between weather, hawks, owls, coyotes, man and many other factors these mighty birds have a hard time surviving. Our hats are off to the Turkey Federation who work very hard to distribute tons of corn each year to help the turkeys make it through the winters.

Over the years we have scored on a lot of turkeys and Smoky, Frank, Paul, Arnie and I have shot the majority of them. And don't believe the statement that you can't drive turkeys to a fellow hunter. Knowing the lay of the land and taking advantage of different situations we have scored this way quite a few times!

Gray Wolf in turkey blind with a nice tom in 1995.

MUSHROOMING

Every spring about a week after Mother's Day we get another bonus from our Deer Camp. When the trillium blossom in the woods the morel mushrooms begin to make their annual appearance. First up are the black morels, closely followed by the gray and white. Mushrooming is almost as much fun as deer hunting and we spend many happy hours seeking this bonus crop.

After picking the highly coveted fungus, most of us cut them up, sun dry them on a screen and store them in jars. They seem to keep forever this way. All you have to do then is soak them in water and they are ready to be cooked. Fried in butter, stuffed with sausage or cut up in an omelet, they simply can't be beat.

Mushroom pickers though are far worse at trespassing than deer hunters are, hands down. They leave cans, bottles and trash including cigarette butts all over the woods. Both local residents and tourists from all over the Midwest and Canada seem to lose all respect for private and State property in search for this natural delicacy. Fresh morels can fetch around $30 per pound in some markets! Fences and signs do not deter them either. In jest, maybe we should have either an open season or bounty on trespassing mushroomers!

During the mushroom season we have a work bee at the Eight Ball Camp and most of our members come up for a long weekend. We work half a day mending fences, cutting wood, painting and cleaning up the roads, etc., then the rest of the day we hunt mushrooms. Bob Thomas, who helps us with our work from spring until deer season, has coined a new description of mushrooming. He calls it "Goonie Hunting". But whatever you call it, we surely love it and many times throughout the year those "Goonies" really make the meals super special!

What's not to love? Gray Wolf with 8-1/2 and 10-1/2 inch white morels (above) in 1995.

Below: Two nice baskets from May 2000.

Drummond Island Spring Trip

One spring Denny Wenzel and Jim Bellamy drove up from Sparta, Michigan to Gaylord to be met by Norb Tutlass, and Dwayne Bellows who were both from Traverse City. Denny and Jim both worked for Spartan Distributors which sold Toro lawn mowers, leaf blowers, snow blowers and the like. Dwayne was a Toro dealer in Traverse City, which is about 60 miles southwest of Gaylord, and Norb was the Vice-President of a bank in Traverse City. I was a Toro dealer at Don's Sport & Marine on Otsego Lake. We hit it off at the dealer meetings and spent many days fishing together and enjoying one another's company.

This trip we loaded our gear into two vehicles and off we headed across the Mackinaw Bridge between the Upper and Lower Peninsula, then north and east to the Drummond Island ferry.

Denny had booked us at the Way-Wen Resort cottages and we settled into the cabin, anticipating all the fish we were going to catch. After a couple of Jim Beam and water medicines we got into our usual nickel and dime limit poker games. It is amazing how five businessmen can sit down and thoroughly enjoy one another's company like this, and completely forget about all the stress of trying to make a living as businessmen.

Over the years we have spent many vacations like this and treasure every one of them. Fish or no fish, it was always a pleasure to spend a few days together. It was usually a spring trip and then again ice fishing a few times each year.

We were up at dawn, and after devouring a big breakfast cooked by our "chef supreme" Denny, we were off to catch some perch or whatever else would bite. The weather was cold and windy, but we were dressed in snow suits, mittens, and Sorrel boots, so we were prepared!

The ice was out of our bay and heading out toward the islands and Lake Huron. We caught some pike and quite a few perch and back to the cabin we went. The owner of the resort told us the smelt were running and the suckers were also in the river spawning. After lunch we put on waders and headed for the river to try and net some suckers for a friend of mine who smokes them.

The stream we went to was about 30 feet wide and up to our hips, and was very fast water. We had a couple of wash tubs that we put on the bank and then into the water we went. All we had to do was hold a big landing net on the bottom and we could feel the suckers hit our nets. It was quite an experience and we filled our tubs which we would empty into the bed of one of the pickups, then go back into the stream for more.

Denny, who played college football at Ferris State, reminded me of a great big grizzly bear. He would put his net on the bottom, then run upstream hollering like a kid at a ball game until his net was full of suckers, then go back to dump them into our wash tubs.

After we had about half of a pickup bed full of suckers, we returned to our cabin and collapsed! After a little nap and a delicious fish supper—complete with American fries, corn, and bean salad—we relaxed for a while. About 9:30 PM that evening, we headed for the tubes that were under the road to the ferry. We had our smelt nets, and after a couple of hours of dipping we had enough fresh smelt for our noon meal the next day, plus quite a bunch to take home.

The next day we followed the ice as it left our bay, and we caught a nice mess of perch which we filleted and froze to take home. The next morning we packed up and headed back to our homes—tired, but very happy guys looking forward to our next trip.

We often fished at Brevort Lake, Indian Lake, Manistique Lake, and Munoscong Bay, all in the Upper Peninsula of Michigan. Regardless of the weather we would go out and usually caught a mess of fish too.

Just business as usual on a spring trip to Drummond Island.

An October trip in the fall of 1975 leaves Gray Wolf with a handful of tasty perch. Denny's son Jeff often accompanied us over the years, and that's him, then age seven, with a few nice fish of his own.

The Wenzel Family

Edythe and I became very good friends of the Wenzel family, and we made several trips down to Rockford, Michigan to spend a couple of days with Denny, Carol and their two sons Jeff and Todd. This relationship led to our inviting them to spend a week with us at our Canadian camp in the wilds. Denny was real anxious to make the trip as were the two boys. Carol also agreed to the adventure, but we were just a wee bit apprehensive as to her reactions of being isolated from town and people for a whole week as she was a BIG CITY GAL.

Finally the day came and Edythe, Carol, Denny and Jeff piled into their van and headed off to Five Mile Lake Lodge, in Ontario. This is a lodge with cabins and a flying service where we pick up groceries and the like before flying into our beloved cabin on Nushatogaini Lake.

It is about a 300 mile trip from Gaylord by car—north to Sault Ste. Marie, Ontario, then 50 miles east to Thessalon, then north again on Highway 129 to Five Mile Lake. The trip takes about six to seven hours, counting stops for breakfast, customs, and for a coke or an ice cream cone. From Thessalon north, this is a very scenic drive. The farm country turns to solid rock and trees and you follow the Missisaugi River most of the time. Occasionally you'll see deer, moose, and bear along the way.

Todd and I climbed into my Piper Super Cruiser float plane and took off from Otsego Lake and headed north. After an hour and twenty minute flight we were met by the Canadian customs agent, then gassed up the plane and took off again for the bush country.

From flat farming country, the land turns to nothing but rock mountains, trees, swamps, and hundreds of lakes of all shapes and sizes. There are no navigational aids other than your compass, map, and just knowing the country. Basically if the weather allows it, we follow the Garden River Valley to Garden Lake, then head northeast to Ranger Lake, north again to Megasin Lake, and finally east to our beautiful Nushatogaini Lake. Total time is usually two and a half to three hours.

The weather was good and we landed and tied up our plane at one of our two docks. We unloaded our gear and opened up camp—ready for the arrival for the rest of our crew. Our very good friend and owner of the Five Mile Lodge flew the rest of our crew and all of their gear and supplies in for the next week. During our vacations we very seldom ever see another soul until Frank flies in to fly out the bunch, gear, and fish.

Our gang flew in early in the afternoon and we proceeded to settle into the camp. Jeff found a baby cottontail rabbit under the cabin and the rabbit, never having seen a human before, allowed him to pick it up and pet it in the palm of his hand. This was a new adventure for the Wenzels and we knew Denny and the boys would adapt well, but again we all were concerned for Carol. Well, she fooled us by really falling in love with bush life and all it has to offer.

We caught mostly northern pike all that week—so plentiful were they that we made a rule not to keep anything under 30 inches. Our most productive fishing day came on a downstream trip where it rained so hard all day that we had to continuously bail out the canoes with Folgers coffee cans. On another trip downstream that week, Carol about went out the backside of the canoe as a big 20-pound lunker pike came out of the water directly at her as she reeled in her blue and silver Creek Chub. Her eyes still get wild when we recall that story, and she laughs about it with a hint of fear still in her voice. She swears she was going to be eaten by that pike, sitting right there in the middle of that canoe!

While bobber fishing with large shiner minnows at sunset one evening, Denny literally had to hold eight year old Todd down in his seat to keep him from being pulled from the boat, as he fought a monster pike. All the while, Edythe, Jeff and I watched with smiles from the other boat. It was a wonderful trip that we all still talk about as we've kept in touch with one another over the years.

Carol "The Big City Gal" and a dandy pike in front of our cabin.

Shorty and Gray Wolf in 1984 with artwork Jeff had made after their first trip to Nusha'.

Jeff, Todd, and Denny with Shorty in the background on their first trip in 1980.

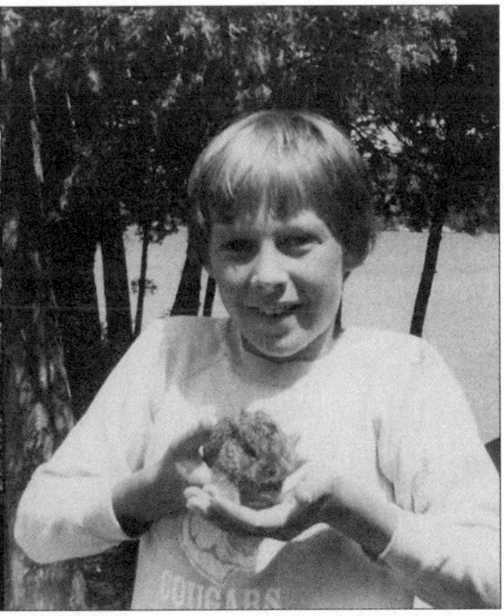

Jeff with a baby cottontail we found under the cabin when we first broke camp.

Father & Son Trips

Each year since Butch was eighteen years old we have flown to our cabin in Canada. Butch does most of the flying on these trips which gives him enough flying time to keep from getting rusty. We have run into all different types of weather and on several occasions had to land on different lakes to let storms go by, or to let the fog clear so we could continue on our way. Each trip has been different and they all bring back memories.

One year Edythe and I flew our plane and Butch flew with his sister Donna in a borrowed plane we call The Green House. It was a green Super Cub that had the whole cockpit made of clear plastic. It was quite a setup that gave the pilot and his passenger a beautiful view. Donna was very uncomfortable in this plane and got air sick, so on the return trip I ended up flying Donna home and Butch flew his mother back to home base.

This was quite a trip. We flew both planes to Chapleau, Ontario where we landed in the river. We tied up the planes and walked to town to do our shopping, then on to Nusha'. Once we settled in at camp, Butch and I went fishing and found a bay that every time we went north we would catch a couple of nice pike, but going south we caught nothing.

Well, we stopped and anchored and cast out bobbers with big minnows on a steel-leadered hook, and we really hit the jackpot. We caught and released all kinds of pike to the point that the inside of the boat was slippery and hard to keep our footing. We were laughing like a couple of kids, really enjoying ourselves. It got so rough we finally had to quit and go home to poach fish for supper, which is my favorite way to cook them.

You need a big cast iron frying pan and you cover the bottom of the pan with milk and a bunch of sliced onions. Take your fillets and use garlic salt and mixed spices on both sides. Lay them on top of the onions and cover the pan. Let it cook just two to three minutes and then turn over the fish. Cover the pan again and cook for another few minutes, and VOILA!, you have some of the best eating this side of Heaven. Try it on any kind of fish and you will be pleasantly surprised!

The next September, Butch and I flew up just the two of us for a four to five day trip. We took a pleasant canoe trip way down to the eighth lake on our water course where I had noticed some nice brook trout spawning there on the previous moose hunt. We anchored upstream from a nice big pool, and I took out a big Mepps spinner and a gob of nightcrawlers. Butch laughed at me and said, "No brook trout will hit a big bait like that."

But after watching me catch two beauties about 16-inches long, he quit laughing and switched to the same type of lure. I have never before, or since, seen such a beautiful catch of brookies. We limited out and never kept one less than 14-inches long. They were so highly colored that they looked like they were bleeding when we flipped them into our canoe. These episodes really come out of our memory books quite often.

We had heard that Graveyard Lake about 20 miles north and west of our lake was producing some good walleye and pike fishing, so Butch and I decided to try it out. We loaded our rods and some tackle into our plane and away we went. There was an old abandoned saw mill at the west end of the lake and as we approached for a fly-by we noticed several logs floating in the lake. After circling twice, Butch picked a spot to land and as we dropped over the trees a big cow moose looked up at us—probably wondering what we were.

After landing we taxied up to a small stream that was flowing into the lake, threw out our anchor and commenced fishing. Butch cast out and BINGO, he landed a nice five pound walleye. I crawled over onto the other pontoon and flipped out a Dardevle and just started a jerking retrieve when WHAM, I latched onto a pike who wasted no time in showing me he had no intentions of ending up on our stringer. I fought him just long enough to see the fish and he broke my line—and for all I know, he is still breaking lines.

We ended up with several nice walleye and pike, and threw them into a burlap bag and off we flew back to

Nushatogaini Lake. We returned to the same spot twice and never even got a strike! That's how fishing goes, even in Canada. One day you could fill the boat with fish, and the next it is hard to even get a strike.

We missed our father and son trip in 1996 as Butch was very sick, and seemed to keep going downhill physically. The doctors were treating him for gout until finally they realized he was having kidney failure. We almost lost Butch.

He was put on a home dialysis program which did help and he started to gain some weight back. He began to feel a little better, but what a terrible way to have to live. He was hooked up to a machine all night and had to take a lot of medication. His only hope of ever leading a normal life was a kidney transplant. I offered mine, but at 76 they do not take organs from anyone my age. Finally after waiting several months, they found out that Butch's wife Joyce was a match and she generously offered to give our son one of her kidneys. It was a gift of life and a great sacrifice on Joyce's part.

They both went to the University of Michigan Hospital in Ann Arbor where the operation was performed. They both weathered the procedure and Joyce was allowed to come home after about five days. Butch's stay was about 12 days and we had to drive back and forth for check-ups every week for quite some time. Then it went to every two weeks, then once a month, then every three months, and finally every four months. This was truly an answer to prayer and Butch now looks and feels great. Thanks to God, Joyce, the surgeons and post-Op team, we again have a healthy son.

In September of 1997, we set off once again to our

Shangri-la in Canada. Butch, his two brother-in-laws—twin brothers, Bob and Bill Brown—and I headed off to Nushatogaini Lake for five days of relaxation and fishing. Bill and Bob fished in one boat and Butch and I in another. We have a standing bet on the longest walleye and the longest pike—.50 cents on each category, each day. It seems to work out that no one loses too much money and it is a lot of fun!

We caught lots of walleye and pike and also caught three very nice lake trout. We eat like kings while in camp which usually includes fresh fish at least three times. Both Butch and Bill like to cook and Bob and I wash dishes and keep the camp clean. Since the Canadians are making moose hunting almost impossible for non-residents, and the fact that my hunting partners and I are getting too old for those rigorous hunts, our father and son trips in September get the job of winterizing and closing up camp.

This is quite a lot of work and kind of sad too, but it has to be done. We drain our shower, water pump, and all the outboards, as well as change the oil in their lower units and fog out the engines. We pull out our boats, and put in the snow load pole on the main center log of the cabin so the snow won't collapse our roof. Out go the bear pads and window shutters, and finally we drain the outside jon.

All of our gear and fish get packed up, and we put any freezable groceries in our pits in the ground before we thoroughly clean the cabin. After all of this we wait for the Beaver aircraft to come and pick us up for the return trip to civilization. Once home, we start counting the days to return the next spring!

Butch and Gray Wolf, making memories on our annual trip to Nusha' in 1999.

Butch, Gray Wolf and Don Huff. Taking a lunch break down river.

Walk Out

This story happened to take place on my 50th birthday. Our group of six had been flown to our cabin to hunt for moose. Willy Peterson flew us in his 180 Cessna float plane with the understanding that he was to pick us up and fly us back to Flame Lake on November 1st.

We had a great week of hunting, fishing, and pinochle playing. We had shot three moose and a lot of our time was spent cutting up the animals and hauling them back to camp. The weather was cold, but nice and sunny. The beavers were working overtime hauling birch and poplar branches for their winter food. They anchor the butts of the branches in the bottom of the lake close to their houses so they can swim out under the ice, cut the branches and haul them into their houses to chew off the bark for their tasty meals. The ducks and geese were heading south as Old Man Winter was getting ready to take over the Northwoods.

November 1st was bright and sunny and we waited all day for Willy to fly us, our moose, and our gear back to our trucks at Flame Lake—but no Willy! November 2nd was cloudy, but still a good day to fly and Willy did not show up again. Needless to say, we could not understand what was holding him. Willy is a good pilot, but takes a lot of chances. Was he having mechanical trouble, sick, or possibly crashed on one of the mountains?

Having no means of communication, a person can think of all kinds of things that could have happened. We were back in the bush about 25 miles from the closest road and the country is very rough, with swamps, rivers, dense woods and rocky hills. November 3rd was again a brisk, clear day. After much discussion we decided that if Willy did not show up that day, Emil (my pinochle partner) and I would attempt to walk out and find out what the problem was. I knew the country better than any of the others as I had hunted not too far from Flame Lake two years before, and both Emil and I were in better physical shape than the others.

Willy did not show up again, so we planned our walk-out escapade. We got up before daylight on my birthday November 4th, had a big breakfast and packed a lunch for both of us. Into our backpacks went a change of clothes, a first-aid kit, a rope, a bush axe, matches, and two compasses. We then loaded our back packs and rifles into one of our canoes that was mounted with a 2-1/2 horse Johnson outboard, and set out in the dark heading south on our lake. We hoped to make it to Flame Lake by nightfall.

We carried our gear and motor across the portage to the start of our river trip. After putting our gear and motor in and onto a different canoe we headed south through lakes One through Four and arrived at the rapids. After portaging our gear again, we traveled south about a quarter-mile and then headed east through a winding creek and over two beaver dams to Black Duck Lake. We crossed the lake to the east end where we hauled the canoe into the brush and put paddles, cushions, motor and gas can under the canoe. It was breaking day, crisp and clear. We had about two to three inches of snow on the ground, and the woods were really beautiful.

I set a compass course for the Aubinadong River and hopefully close to a bridge. After a short walk we came to a small stream that we had to cross. We found a snow covered tree that had bridged the stream, so we decided to cross it. I had my backpack on and a stick in my right hand, with my rifle slung across my left shoulder. I was almost to the other side when my rifle butt hung up on a branch making me lose my balance. I jumped for the bank and almost made it, but my right leg landed in the water.

About this time Emil was laughing his head off at me. I turned on my back and drained the water from my boot and waited for Emil to cross. I asked him what he would have done if I had broken my leg, and his response was, "Guess I would have to shoot you and go on."

My answer was, "Thanks, I'll be sure to return the favor if you get into trouble!"

I would pick out some landmark and Emil would stand behind me to verify the course. Sometimes we would have to deviate and make detours due to the landscape to get our mark, but so far, so good.

While going through some woods we came upon a clearing that was all torn up—ground, trees and all, and the entire area had a very strong odor. This was a place where two bull moose had fought, possibly for the favor of a cow moose standing by waiting for the winner to mate with.

We had to cross a muskeg to get to our next point and we were part way across when we came across a narrow but deep creek. Emil went left and I went right both looking for a crossing, when I heard Emil holler "sonofa—!" followed by a big splash! Guess who laughed then! I found a place where the creek narrowed and jumped across, and then walked back to Emil who was in the process of wringing out his clothes and redressing.

About noon we decided to have a sandwich, so we found a nice spot with rocks to sit on. About half-way through our sandwich we felt our muscles tightening up so we finished our meal walking. Late in the afternoon we had to slide down a big rock formation, practically on our butts, and followed that with a trek through a swamp. Just as the sun was setting we came out to the Aubinadong River and there, just upstream about 200 yards, was the old bridge we had been shooting for. It was not in very good shape, but being careful we made it across to the Old Trail Road where we had hunted a couple of years earlier.

We ran into fog as it got dark, but our target was only three miles to go. Just before Highway 129 on the south side of the road there is a big radio tower we were shooting for, but it was so foggy that we never did see it.

Shortly after we hit the highway, a pickup truck stopped to see if he could help us. After hearing our story, he felt sorry for us and drove us right to Willy's home base at Flame Lake. Neither Willy or a road crew of Indians could believe what we had accomplished, BUT WE DID IT!

After drying our clothes in front of the fireplace and having a good meal that Willy's wife Maureen had made for us, we got into Emil's truck and drove all the way home—250 miles to Gaylord, Michigan. What a birthday it had been!

Willy had been fog bound for four days and could not fly, but the next morning was bright and clear, and he made several trips to Nushatogaini Lake to fly out our buddies, gear, and moose. Thus ending another good moose trip. Our walk-out trip is still being talked about in the Chapleau, Ontario area.

Bob's Moose Hunting Trips

Our son-in-law, Bob King, who has his doctorate in Aquatic Biology and taught at Central Michigan University at Mt. Pleasant, came up for moose hunting with our crew. He and I teamed up as partners that year to shoot an elusive moose. It was a nice day, and we were down river just below the first rapids when I happened to see an antler in some brush just ahead of us. I put the canoe against the bank and pointed to the moose, which by now was moving away from us. Bob fired three shots and the moose was running now. I snapped one more shot and the moose kept running.

We jumped into the canoe and headed down river to a small marsh/lake where the moose seemed to be headed. We beached the canoe and were looking for a possible blood trail when Bob said, "There he is," and maybe 75 yards away, standing facing us was the moose. He was hit on his right side and you could see the blood running out of his wound and from his nose.

Lo and behold he charged us, and I hollered, "Shoot! Shoot!" and Bob's answer was, "I can't—my gun's empty!" About this time I stepped over and shot once more and down he went with a big splash in the marsh grass! He had only one antler, but it was a nice one!

We took off our jackets, rolled up our sleeves and commenced dressing out Bob's moose. While he held the hind leg up I gutted out the bull. I put the heart, tongue, and liver in the canoe, and propped the carcass open covering the opening with spruce boughs. We then had sandwiches and a bottle of O'Keefes Ale, thoroughly enjoying all the beautiful surroundings and the success of shooting a nice bull moose.

The following day we arrived with some help, meat saws, knives and stockinette. It took the four of us a

Bob is all smiles with his one antlered bull from 1973, just below Black Duck Lake.

couple of hours to finish the job and we arrived back in camp with about eight bags of nice clean moose meat. Needless to say we had a huge supper of moose tenderloin with all the trimmings that night. I believe we ended up with another moose that year, so we all had plenty of meat for our freezers once more.

The next year Bob and I walked into a small pond and sat for several hours, but no moose. Lots of tracks and sign, but no moose. It had snowed the day before, and retracing our tracks back to the canoe we saw where a timber wolf had followed us to the little lake but we never did see him!

For the afternoon hunt we went down river to hunt a swampy area and as we got out of the canoe we came upon some moose dung that was still steaming. You guessed it, off we went in pursuit. I am sure those two moose knew we were following them, because they took a very erratic course through the swamp. It went up over a couple of rocky hills, through some very thick Jack Pine and, you guessed it, the trail turned back north just before hitting the river. They crossed their original tracks within 50 yards of our canoe! If it ever happened again, one of us is staying with the canoe while the other takes the trail! It just goes to show that you don't always get your quarry.

Hopefully there will be moose for our grandchildren to hunt. Our area has been declared a Wilderness Area, so there should be no more encroachment like logging roads or bridges. Just one big block of land where you can be part of the wonderful country. You will never be closer to God and all the wonders He has created while you enjoy the good old Nushatogaini River and Lakes watershed.

On another trip Ron Dickerson and I flew our own planes into camp and made several trips to Five Mile Lake, bringing in our buddies and gear. We were at camp a day ahead of the season so we all relaxed and fished, and consequently had fresh walleye with all the trimmings for supper that night.

The next day we all went down river—our son-in-law Bob, and Bob Caras in one canoe; Bud Buller our gunsmith, and Gary Huddleson who delivered our bait to our Sport Shop, in the second canoe; Emil and I made up canoe number three. We split up each canoe where each man wanted to hunt. Emil and I went way down river to the last lake just before the second rapids. We would paddle a little and then float along, and I would call with my homemade birch-bark horn—listening for a short time and then paddling a little farther.

As we nosed around a corner just coming into the last lake, we spotted a nice bull feeding on some lily pad roots. We backed the canoe up, then beached it and tied it up. After a short sneak through the brush, there was our moose about 100 yards away. He had moved in toward shore and was eating some marsh grass. What a beautiful sight he was standing facing us, with the sun glinting off his antlers, and not aware of the fact that he was about to get a one way ticket to moose heaven.

We laid down to get a good position for shooting and at the count of three we both fired. To our surprise the moose did not fall down, but he kicked into high gear and came full tilt right at us. I am sure he never knew we were there because we were in the prone position, hidden from him behind a small knoll. What a gorgeous sight to see the moose running in about a foot of water and it spraying all around him.

Both Emil and I shot a couple more times and the bull collapsed, really making a big splash and he never moved again. I really think we both hit him in the heart and lung area on our first shots and that the moose just ran until he died, because he had two holes in his chest and not another mark on him. We got our block and tackle from the canoe and after toasting the bull with a bottle of ale, we proceeded to dress out our trophy.

After removing all his innards, I asked Emil to find a rock so I could split his itch bone by pounding on my knife. Our knives are handmade out of a special quarter-inch steel and are shaped like a big Russel knife, and they really hold their edge. A moose's quarter-inch hide is murder on a regular knife! Emil came back and handed me a rock with the comment, "I found something better than a rock," and handed me an old .32-40 Winchester that had been propped against a big rock. All the wood had rotted out and the gun was still loaded. It had the barrel sawed off and was probably an old trappers gun.

We went back and dug down where Emil had found the gun and we found the old butt plate about six inches in the dirt. We searched for human bones or the remains of a canoe, but to no avail. We checked with the Canadian Mounties later, but found out nothing. I feel that a trapper crawled into the brush to get away from a storm and probably died right there. The wolves probably ate him, as nobody would leave a rifle like that and just walk away. Kind of a creepy feeling. Can you come up with a better solution?

We hung the moose against a big dead pine tree and

proceeded to head for home. While making the portage around the rapids, we joined with our buddies. After telling our story to them, we headed for home—Bud and Gary in the lead canoe, the two Bob's in the middle, and Emil and I brought up the rear.

As we were leaving the fourth lake I noticed that the two Bobs headed into a bay to our left. As we cleared the point they had shut off the motor and were paddling towards shore where a big cow moose was busy eating lily pad roots. We shut off our motor and then sat back to watch.

Bob shot from the front of the canoe and hit the cow really hard and was about to shoot again when Gary and Bud opened up—both shooting across the two Bobs! Bob quickly shot again and killed the cow. As Gary and Bud came close to the first canoe I never have heard a better butt chewing in all my life for shooting across in front of the first canoe. Emil and I finished what was not said in the first butt chewing and sent them home alone. Boy, what a stupid trick to pull!

Emil and I helped Bob and Bob pull the moose out of the water where we dressed it out and then headed home. There were a couple of toasts to the two moose we had killed, followed by supper and a couple of pinochle games and then off to sleep. The next day we all went back down river and cut up and bagged our two moose. Bud and Gary came along—minus their rifles—and neither one of them was ever asked back to our camp for hunting or fishing. I flew out the two moose to Five Mile Camp and Bob and I flew back to Gaylord while Frank came and flew out the remaining gear...another 355 days until the next moose season.

Winter Flying In Canada

Flying with skis on your plane during the winter was my second choice of fun flying. My first love was float flying and lastly was with wheels. Your plane is much lighter with skis and consequently flew faster in flight. Take offs and landings were also much quicker under normal conditions.

When we were younger we enjoyed flying into our camp in Canada, but you had to adapt to the conditions or you could get into trouble quickly. We never flew into the bush unless we had at least two planes. Without radio communications you had to fly by keeping track of one another visually.

Whenever we landed on lakes, which was 90 percent of the time, we would make a press landing—namely coming down and pressing your skis into the snow, then making a go-round and look at your tracks. If they turned black it indicated that there was slush under the snow, so you would try another place before landing. We would then taxi up to the shore and put logs under the skis so the planes did not freeze down.

The next step would be to drain the oil into empty gas cans and bring them into the cabin, to make the engines easier to start. Next we rigged canvas over our cowlings and then down to the ground like a little tent. We then took burners from old propane stoves and, along with a 20-pound propane cylinder, we would light the burner which was inserted into a three foot length of stove pipe. We then had a regular heat torch!

When it got down to 30 to 40 degrees below zero you could hang on the propeller and it would not budge, and back then we had no electric starters so we had to hand prop the propeller to start the engines. When it heated up to the point that we could hear our magnetos click we would get our oil that we had preheated on our wood stove and pour the warm oil back into our engines. The planes would start right up, and after a short warm up they were ready to fly again.

We took an old Evinrude wide track snowmobile apart and flew it into camp in pieces, then we reassembled it. Instead of having to snowshoe every place we went, we used the old Heavy Evvie as transportation. We always carried two pairs of snowshoes tied to the struts of the plane, plus survival gear, food, blankets, compasses, hatchets, waterproof matches, and a small cooking outfit. To this day I still carry a good knife, waterproof matches, a compass, and bug dope, just in case of a forced landing!

We always caught lots of fish using a hand ice auger

and spud to make the holes, and tip-ups as fishing gear. It was great fun to build a big fire and cook weiners and coffee, and watch the flags on the tip-ups pop into the air. Then it was a race to see who could get there first!

We were very fortunate on our winter trips to Canada. No one got hurt and our planes never let us down. The last trip we made I had a radio in my Super Cruiser, but the other plane did not. On our way home, as we neared our destination, Sault Ste. Marie, Ontario, I was advised we could not land at the airport because there was no snow. The customs said they would meet us on the river and for us to land on the ice, so we headed to the designated spot.

It was a glare of ice with no snow at all. I could see the customs man out on the end of a big pier and I circled, checking out the area. The ice looked real spooky, real dark and slippery, so I approached very slowly almost to a stall speed and as close to shore as possible. I touched down about a quarter of a mile from the pier and slowly eased up to it as it was real slippery and hard to control the plane.

Sandy Storing was piloting the second plane and having no radio he followed me, but touched down too short and too fast. Consequently, when he contacted the ice he could not control his plane too well and he went sliding right past the pier at about 50 miles per hour. Luckily there was a lot of river and he finally slowed down, got out to turn the plane around and made it to where we were waiting. After being checked out we took off and headed to home base, the Otsego County Airport.

We made one last trip in the winter of 1980, I believe. There were five of us and instead of taking our planes, we drove to WaWa, Ontario, and chartered a Beaver Aircraft to fly us in. The pilot had never been in our area so we helped him find our lake. He landed way out in the middle of the lake and would not go anywhere near shore for fear of slush, so we had to carry our gear to the cabin.

Boy was it cold! We made a fire in our wood stove and also our propane gas space heater, and finally thawed out the cabin and us. After a while we got out our old wide track snowmobile and brought the rest of our gear into camp. We had good fishing and used the snowmobile to pack down the snow for a landing strip for when our pilot would return.

It got down to 40 degrees below zero at night, and it was just beautiful. The stars hung in the sky like clusters of grapes, and the Northern Lights danced all through the sky. It was so cold you could hear the trees pop just like rifle shots. The only thing that was not too pleasant were the trips one made to the outdoor jon. The seat was frosty and cold, making these trips very short stops.

The day we were to leave broke nice and clear with the sun sparkling on the snow like a field of diamonds. The Beaver Aircraft arrived, and seeing the runway we made for him, he taxied right up to our island making it much easier to load. The flight was pretty, flying over the lakes and mountains, and we even got to see several moose that had yarded up on the high hills for the winter. That was our last trip to the cabin during the winter months, but we still have many pleasant memories of our winter excursions and they will remain with us until we make our last flight to Heaven!

Ice Fishing

What makes a person roll out of a nice warm bed and get all excited about going out in the cold just to sit on the ice of a frozen lake and stare down at a small bobber in the hopes that a fish will take his bait? You have to be just a little crazy to enjoy brutalizing yourself like this, but we thoroughly enjoy ice fishing, and go at least once every week in the search of a mess of perch. Maybe it is spending the whole day with your buddies or the thrill of watching the sun coming up over the trees on a sparkling white landscape, or maybe it's the anticipation of that little tug on the end of your line. Who knows?

The advance in cold weather clothing, good rods and reels, snowmobiles and four-wheelers to carry you and your gear to your favorite fishing spots, power augers to drill your holes through more than 30 inches of ice, and nice portable shanties all make these experiences much more enjoyable.

My partner in real estate, Don Huff, and his brother Richard, along with myself and Al Beaulieu, a retired school teacher, were the regulars. Then there were Jim Bellamy and Denny Wenzel from Sparta, Michigan who would travel all the way up north to Higgins Lake for a day of companionship and hopefully some fish to take home with them.

We would fish as shallow as eight feet of water to as deep as 50 feet, trying to outsmart those little rascals and usually end up with enough for a couple of good meals for each of us. Every once in a while we would catch a lake trout, pike, sucker, and even some smelt.

Over the years we have had a lot of pleasant trips and memories. One unforgettable trip was in late March and only Don Huff and I were going. It was probably our last trip of the season before the spring break-up. It was a beautiful day and we snowmobiled to our favorite spot along with our sled and gear for a great day of fishing at Higgins Lake. The fish were biting good, but for some reason we did not see any other fishermen. Late in the afternoon we packed up and headed for our truck at the landing.

I was driving and Don was riding on the back of our ice sled when all of a sudden there was open water ahead. I swung the sled around and went back to where we had been fishing, hoping that the ice would be better at the south end of the island. This explained why we had not seen any other fishermen! The lake was breaking up and the ice was shifting with the wind. We managed to get to the south end of the island only to find about a three foot crack in the ice, which separated two ice flows.

I circled around and got some speed up and skipped across the water to the ice, and it looked like we could make shore. We did get about 50 to 60 feet from shore, then it was open water to the land. We now were as close as we were going to get, and under the ice there was only about three feet of water.

Don jumped in and waded to shore and I was hoping our snowmobile and sled would skim over the water if I could get up enough speed. We had seen this done on TV, but not hauling a cargo sled! I made a big circle, then gave our trusty snowmobile full throttle and headed for shore.

It was a strange feeling heading for open water, but we hit with a splash and skimmed over the water towards the shore. We hit the beach with a bang, but we were on sound footing. The beach was sand and the roads were bare of snow, so Don walked back at least three-fourths of a mile to get the truck. We loaded up and headed for home, much the wiser on what to look for when it is near the last ice!

Thawing out with Don Huff.

Fishing Buddy Jim Bellamy.

Bungalow Ice Fishing

Don Huff, his brother Richard, and his son-in-law Mark and I will go just about anywhere ice fishing to catch perch and walleyes. We heard and read about "Bungalow" ice fishing and decided to give it a try. We called from an ad in one of the sporting magazines to a place at Lake Nipissing, which is at North Bay, Ontario. The man's name behind the bungalows is Dennis Johnson. He has several of them, which he puts out on the lake and rents them to avid fishermen from freeze up all winter until the ice gets down to about 12-inches thick. At this point he hauls them back to shore until the next year.

We rented one of the bungalows for three nights in mid January 1998 and at 6 AM in the brisk winter air we were off for a new adventure. We left Gaylord in my Suburban with two snowmobiles on our trailer and headed north to St. Ignace, Michigan, which is where we picked up Mark. From there we made it through customs at the Soo and took Highway 17 east to North Bay, Ontario. After a 10 hour drive we finally arrived at Lake Nipissing which is about 30 miles long itself. We arrived at the Johnson Resort late in the afternoon and drove out on the ice about three miles to the bungalows.

Ours was about 10x14 feet, consisting of one big room with six bunk beds, a sink, refrigerator, table and chairs, and a nice gas wall heater which kept the place nice and warm. There were 6 to 10 holes cut in front of the bunks, all with removable covers. You could sit or lie on the beds and fish right inside the bungalow in solid comfort, or you could drill holes outside—whatever turned you on.

We were late getting settled but did fish a little bit that first day, just for the novelty of the situation. We caught a couple of whitefish and missed a few bites too. When we turned out the lights it took all of about six seconds and we were all fast asleep. We were all bushed from the 10 hour drive which was very little expressway driving—most of it was double-lane highway which is tough driving in the winter.

The next morning we were all up before dawn like a bunch of kids on Christmas morning! The temperature outside was around 0 degrees Fahrenheit. Our bathroom was a hook-onto-the-cabin structure about three foot square with a gas light burning 24 hours a day to keep it warm—quite functional, but not too comfortable. Needless to say our trips to the bathroom were quite short in time!

We fished around the cabin most of the first day and

we caught a few walleyes, whitefish and perch, but nothing like we expected. Dennis, the owner of the bungalows stepped out and brought us a fresh supply of water as well as minnows for fishing. He is a private pilot, just as I am and we became pretty good friends after swapping experiences. We conveyed our disappointment in the fishing, so he said he would show us one of his personal fishing spots.

Dennis arrived early the next morning in near blizzard conditions. He had his four-wheel drive vehicle and took Don Huff and I on a trip we will remember for the rest of our lives! It was snowing so hard most of the time we could not see over 100 yards as we hugged the shoreline going over several pressure cracks. Ten miles and an hour later we stopped at what appeared to be a big rock pile.

We drilled three or four holes in the ice, which was well over 24 inches thick and building more every day. I hunched down with my back to the storm and my butt on a six-gallon pail and proceeded to try to catch a fish. Dennis parked his vehicle crossways to the wind and drilled a hole by each back door—this way Donnie, who was having trouble with his breathing, could sit in the vehicle and watch his line. We did catch a few nice walleye, pike and perch, and then decided we should go back to camp as Den was planning a trip the next day with a group of his customers who were not having very good luck either.

The next day was a nice one. We had a group of maybe 20 guys driving several trucks and four snowmobiles to the honey hole. Richard and Mark took snowmobiles and we took my Suburban and a portable shanty for Don, and away we went. Upon arriving at our spot everyone spread out, drilled a bunch of holes and commenced catching fish. We put up the shanty for Donnie, augured more holes fairly close by and started some serious fishing.

Donnie was about 30 feet from me and was catching walleyes and now and then a pike or perch. I was catching some very nice perch with the odd walleye and pike. We all caught our limits and also hooked into some lunkers that broke our poles and got away. All in all, it was a fantastic day of fishing. After going back to the bungalow for a fresh fish fry with all the trimmings, we cleaned and packed fish for our trip home the next day.

We were up at daylight and it was very still outside and 18 degrees below zero. The Suburban started right up and after a little coaxing so did our trusty Polaris snowmobiles. We then hooked up our trailer and headed for home. In all, it was a very different trip and bungalow fishing is A-OK in our book. The Good Lord willing, we will try it again some day.

Dennis, the owner, and his family are super people and he has the roads all plowed out about 40 feet wide and as smooth as pavement to make it easy for his guests. Our trip home was made without any trouble and all of us arrived safe and sound, but very tired. All ice fishermen have to be a little crazy to brutalize ourselves like we do, but we have good equipment and super buddies to enjoy these outings with.

Crash Number Two

In 1995, my good buddy and partner, Don Huff, had flown up to camp with me in my Piper Super Cruiser for a few days of fishing, and returned from our trip on June 19, (my mother's birthday). We were coming in for a landing at Airdale Seaplane Base for customs and gas for the plane as I had been doing for 33 years. At the touchdown on contact with the water my right float suddenly let go and flipped over to the right—immediately at 70 MPH the plane flipped up and we were heading for the bottom of the river in about 35 feet of water.

I cut the switches and unbuckled my safety belt and was curling up in a ball to kick out the windshield when the door of the plane opened. Being completely under water I squirmed out of there like an otter, grabbing my wife's cookie tin that floated by as I went out the door.

The float was hanging to the plane by some guy wires, so I grabbed the float and helped Donnie out and onto it. We had a hard time getting his flotation jacket out of the cabin as it was wedged up against the ceiling, but finally out it came. Only by the grace of God were we saved from a watery grave that day.

Some people at Sugar Island witnessed the crash and immediately jumped onto their pontoon boat and came to our rescue. They took us to their home and wrapped us with blankets and gave us hot coffee to prevent hypothermia. Someone called 911 and shortly the EMTs were there to check us out physically. Outside of the trauma of the crash and a few cuts and bruises, we seemed to be OK, again thank God!

This accident was on TV and in all the local papers. It was classified as an International accident due to the fact that the river is the boundary line between Canada and the United States. The US Coast Guard came over to where we were and gave me a ticket that cost $50 for submerging an engine in the river. We never even left an oil slick, and their two big outboards on their boat were putting more pollution into the river than we did! They never asked if we were OK and could not have cared less!

On the other hand, the Canadian authorities stayed at the scene all day long and one came over to me and put his arm around my shoulders and said, "We are glad you are both OK and as far as we are concerned the case is closed, and you are cleared to leave." Quite a difference isn't it?

I called Airdale Sea Plane Base which was where we were headed and was only about one mile from where we had had our misfortune, and they sent a crew to recover the sea plane. They dove down and secured flotations to the plane and towed it back to their base. They hired a huge crane and attached a cable to the tail section then slowly raised the plane out of the water. They backed up to dry land and as they let it down we secured a set of wheels like a dolly under the fuselage. It was then towed into their main hangar where the mechanics drained out the oil and gas, removed our bent prop, put on one of their props and started the engine!

Our floats and attachments were ruined and the windshield and another window were broken. There were a few dents in the right wing and wing tip, and a few places too where the fabric was torn. When the right float turned over upon landing, the left float came loose and the prop cut off about two feet of it, ruining the float and the propeller. Our son Butch drove up to Sault Ste. Marie, Ontario and helped with the recovery of the plane, then drove us home late that afternoon.

A couple of weeks later we drove up to Canada with our pontoon trailer and brought back the floats, and a week after that we returned and picked up the fuselage and wings. We put what was left of "Betsy" in our hangar at the airport.

About a month later I sold our faithful old girl to a pilot who lives about forty miles from Gaylord. There sure was a big lump in my throat when we loaded "Betsy" on our trailer and the new owner took it down the road, and to my knowledge today she is still not air worthy. Only by the grace of God are my buddy Don Huff and I still here. Huff is still suffering from injuries to his arm and elbow and I walk with a slight limp, but we are blessed to be here.

We still go to our little piece of heaven at Nushatogaini Lake, but now we drive to Five Mile Lake Lodge and they fly us in. After trying three different radios/antennas, we finally have a means of communication from our camp. We are tied into a radio tower at Chapleau and can only use the phone for six minutes at a time, then we are cut off automatically so others can use the tower.

It was a real thrill for all of us to call home, and our wives could hardly believe that we were talking to them from the bush country! We all feel more comfortable knowing that in case of an accident we will now be able to get any help necessary! This is not a means to visit, but a way to call out for help if needed. In the not too distant future we will be able to use a satellite and call anywhere with no time limit! Just one more miracle of our present day way of living.

My second, and hopefully last, plane crash that I have walked (or swam) away from and lived to tell about.

Ralph's Moose & The Canadians

It was back in about 1975 when Frank Uhaus, our outpost owner at Five Mile Lake, built a cabin on the fourth lake of our river system—so consequently our wilderness was invaded. On the bad side every once in a while we see a boat or two, but on the plus side we have made friends with a particular group of Canadian moose hunters.

They come up every year and we hunt together, each of us respecting one another's favorite spots. They usually come up to our cabin and have supper with us and spend the night at our camp. Just a super bunch of dedicated hunters. We not only have shared our hunting territory, but even moose meat when the occasion presented itself.

In 1989, our good friend Ralph Pichan, a local businessman, was our guest and I hunted with Ralph that year. I had shot my moose the second day out, so we were in a canoe showing my friend some new country. It was a beautiful day and we were thoroughly enjoying every minute of it. After portaging the rapids we came upon three of our Canadian friends at what we call Noon Day Camp. It is a point sticking out in the sixth lake of our river system, and we have a fire pit and a little rustic table built there.

We joined them for lunch and conversation, and after finding out that their luck had been no moose, I jokingly told them that we were going to hunt right across from them on the west bank of the river and kill a moose that was waiting for us. They laughed and said, "Good luck" and off we went.

Unbeknownst to the Canadians, there actually was a meadow on the west side that we called Mating Meadow that could not be seen from the river, but we had shot several moose there on past trips. We beached our canoe and I led Ralph into our hidden meadow of tall grass and willow brush.

We moved very slowly and came to the remains of an old beaver dam, turned the corner and there was a nice bull moose moving away from us. I was not carrying my rifle but pointed out the moose to Ralph saying, "Shoot it, shoot it!" Just as the bull went into the brush, BOOM, Ralph shot but the moose had already disappeared.

I turned to my buddy and said, "What in the heck were you shooting at?" His reply was, "I never saw the bull, but shot at a cow that was standing in the brush on the opposite side of the meadow from the bull."

We made our way over to where Ralph said the cow

ran and sure enough there was a real good blood trail. We sat down for a few minutes and hearing no sound, we followed the blood trail maybe 50 yards and there the cow moose was. She had fallen against a big blown down tree and was propped up on about a 45 degree angle, deader than a two day old smelt.

We dressed the moose out right as it lay, which made it a lot easier to remove the guts. After taking the heart, liver and tongue with us, we returned to our canoe only to be confronted by our Canadian buddies. They could not believe they had sat on their point most of the day without realizing our Mating Meadow ever existed.

We shot our moose, but lost the secrecy of one of our favorite spots. The Canadians moved right in and shot a nice bull there the very next morning. More power to them—it could not happen to a nicer group of hunters!

Left to right: Mac, Ron, and Ralph quartering Ralph's moose on our front dock at the cabin. That's my faithful "Betsy" in the back-ground.

Moose hunter Ralph Pichan.

Winter At Munuscong Bay

Don Huff, his brother Richard and I dearly love to ice fish, especially for perch. We have good equipment—two snowmobiles, a trailer, two power augers, shanties of all types, and we will go just about anywhere in search of the tasty perch.

We get up really early and head across the Mackinac Bridge which is one of the greatest engineering feats of the century. On this suspension bridge are four lanes of traffic connecting the Lower and Upper Penninsulas of Michigan over a stretch of water about five miles across and it is the connecting link of Lake Michigan and Lake Huron.

We always have a large breakfast at a truck stop just out of St. Ignace then go north and east to Cedarville, north of Pickford then east to Munuscong Bay which is a large bay off the St. Mary's River which connects Lake

Superior to Lake Huron.

Our favorite spot is about six miles across the ice to Allard Bay. At no place is it more than six or seven feet deep with about two and a half feet of ice. This does not leave too much depth of water to fish in. We always drill from ten to twenty holes and keep moving until we find some fish, hopefully. We stay at Joe Johnston's Resort and the cabins are small and a bit drafty, but who cares when you are fishing? The tap water smells when it is not frozen so we bring our own water for coffee.

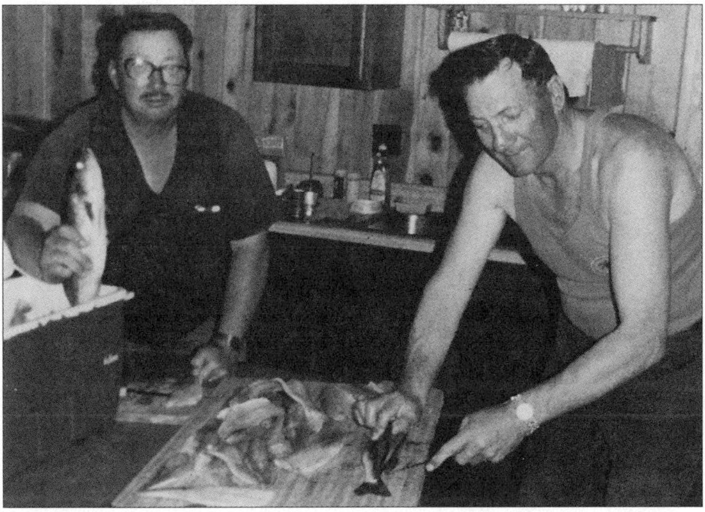

Brothers Richard (left) and Don Huff (right).

Joe has eight cabins and is usually filled up summer and winter. There is a small bait shop and grocery store where all the fishing stories are exchanged. Some true and some not so true! He has a wash-up room and toilets that the people use when their cabin's water systems are frozen up. This is just a real neat place to go and relax while fishing. When the weather is right and the fish cooperate, a lot of walleye, perch, pike and panfish are caught.

We arrived around 10 AM and unpacked, got our snowmobiles unloaded, loaded our gear on our ice sled and across the bay we went. It was a beautiful day though cold, but we were dressed for the occasion so we didn't mind. After drilling our holes we started fishing. Every now and then we would catch a couple, just enough to keep things interesting.

After a while Donnie started hole hopping and whenever he would catch a perch or two and move on I would go to the hole he left and then I would catch a pike. This happened all afternoon. I must have caught thirty pike that day and released them all except a couple of the better ones.

As the sun went down we packed up and headed for the cabin. It was clear as a bell so we knew we were in for a cold night. After getting our gear off the sleds and into the cabin we parked the snowmobiles and had supper, played a little penny-ante poker and the turned into our sleeping bags.

It got down to about fifteen below zero that night and after a big breakfast we went out to start and warm up our snowmobiles. I climbed onto my machine which I had parked facing a big snow bank where Joe had plowed the snow. I pulled out the choke and after pulling the starter over a few times I turned on the key, hit the starter and my machine took off at full throttle. It hit the snow bank and turned to the north wide open.

I had fallen off when it hit the big snow bank and just sat there helpless watching my snowmobile take off heading right for the back of another of Joe's cabins. I was sure that it was going to go right through the wall and tear up everything. But the machine zoomed right up the big snow bank behind the other cabin. It dropped eight feet to the ground and the throttle broke loose to idle position without hurting anything.

The guys came running over to see if I was hurt as I was still sitting down on my butt in the snow. We all went over and got the snowmobile back to our cabin. We started up the other machine and away we went fishing. We caught a nice mess of fish and then it was off for home again until the next time!

Just before spring break-up the same crew was back in the same old cabin to try our luck on the fish again. The trip across the bay was uneventful and we were having a great time. The sun was out and everything was melting. We were enjoying ourselves so much we failed to notice that all the other fishermen had left and we were all alone on the ice. We loaded our sleds with our shanties and gear and we broke through the slush and water and could not pull the sleds as they built up with slush and ice and became too heavy.

I climbed onto the snowmobile and unhooked the sled and found out if I rode alone at a good speed that I could stay on top of the ice. We decided that I should go for help. So off I went, slush and ice flying at full throttle, six miles across the ice to Joe's resort. I pulled into his parking lot and the snowmobile died! It had gotten so hot that it burned a hole through the piston.

There was a group of fishermen from Ohio and they had two Hovercrafts. These machines have a big fan under the body that puts the craft on a cushion of air and can go over dirt, ice, water, swamp or anything else. After hearing my story they went out and picked up our men and gear, and brought them safely back to camp. They would not take a dime for doing a good deed, which renews one's faith that there are still a lot of good people around.

We have been more careful after this episode and watch the weather and conditions much more than we had before. One never knows what will transpire when we head off on our fishing adventures!

Frenchie's Moose

Owen Wuelfing, Frenchie to us, was a great guy. He was a good cook and really loved to go moose hunting. He was a good man in a canoe which is half the battle the way we hunted. No matter what the weather was Frenchie was game to go out, and when the work came of cutting and hauling out the moose he always did his share and never complained about a thing. He dearly loved to fly with me no matter what the weather was either. We lost Frenchie in 1996 after a long bout with the "Big C", and we all miss him very much.

Back a few years ago when Ontario required non-residents to have two licenses for one moose, we had six of us in camp which allowed us to have three moose. It was permissible for any of us to shoot any number of the three moose as long as we did not exceed our three critters. After three days of hunting, not one of us had seen a moose.

Frenchie and I stopped to visit with our Canadian friends from Orillia, Ontario, and their luck had not been very good either. They had killed one bull for six of them in a week's hunting. One of their party had sighted a cow and yearling just to the east of their camp, but they were too far away to take a shot. They were going home that afternoon so Frenchie and I decided to give the area called Little Bean and Big Bean Lake a try the next day.

I knew the area quite well from previous hunts and decided to try Little Bean Lake in the morning. We got there just about daylight and decided to hunt there. Little Bean Lake was mostly marsh grass with a nice little stream running through it that emptied into the Nushatogaini River system to the west. It ran north and south about 100 yards and was probably 400 yards or more across.

We picked a spot on the south side among some nice spruce trees and we made a comfortable spruce bough nest using a tree as a back rest. We packed our lunch and brought a couple of pocket westerns to read, intending to stay all day. Every once in a while I would give a cow moose call, trying to get a moose to react to the call. I was not carrying a gun as it was Frenchie's day.

About 11 AM we spotted a movement in some spruce trees at the east end of the marsh. Shortly after a nice big cow stepped out into the marsh grass that came up to her belly, I whispered to Frenchie to let her come down to the creek for a drink.

Lo and behold out stepped a nice yearling calf who headed to the creek also. It was easily a 200 yard shot or better. When they were both nicely out in the open I said, "Shoot them both and take the cow first." Frenchie replied, "No, I might miss," and handed me the gun which I had never fired before in my life.

I held it about three inches over her back and touched off the rifle. Talk about luck. The cow dropped in her tracks out of sight in the marsh grass. The calf turned and headed for the brush. I shot twice and was sure I had hit it hard on the second shot. All was calm and quiet except for Frenchie. He jumped up and took off his hat waving it up and down and said, "We got them, didn't we buddy!"

After sitting there about ten minutes we picked our way around the edge of the grassy area. We forded the creek at the east end, then walked back to where the cow was. She had died on impact of the hit and was lying in a perfect place to field dress her out.

While Frenchie was admiring our kill, I searched the area where I had shot at the calf and soon found a good blood trail heading for the spruce thicket they had originally come from. I trailed very slowly and spotted the moose standing not more than 20 feet inside the trees not even moving. After moving to get a clear shot I killed it with a neck shot. Two moose both high and dry away from the mud and water. Who could ask for more?

We went right to the task of dressing out both animals. We propped open the body cavities, covered them with spruce boughs and then headed for the cabin. When the others returned empty handed and heard our news, we all had a toast to the moose and prepared to all go back the next day.

We returned to cut up the moose, bagged the pieces

in stockinette and hung them up to cool properly. We brought our canoes up the small river right to the west end of the marsh and only had to pack the meat about 200 yards or so which worked out very well. Being on high ground we skinned out the two moose and used the hide to cut them up on. After hauling the meat to the canoes we loaded all of it into the 17-footer and proceeded to head for camp.

I took a paddle and rope and sat on top of the meat to keep the canoe tracking right. When we got out to the first lake they sped up the outboard and we almost lost the meat and myself as the heavily loaded canoe started taking in water. I finally got the attention of the first canoe and signaled to cut the speed. The canoe followed real well after that and we made it back to the portage without any further trouble. After carrying all the moose meat over the portage to our Nushatogaini Lake we headed back to camp very tired but happy guys.

Moose hunting is a lot of work but I love every facet of it and will miss it very much. My moose hunting buddies are getting too old to take the work that is involved and the Canadian government has made the rules too difficult for non-residents to participate anymore. As I have remarked earlier the once-in-a-lifetime moose hunt developed into going 30 years in a row—a very big chapter in the experiences of Gray Wolf.

Owen Wuelfing or "Frenchie" and Gray Wolf with our cow moose from 1990.

Frenchie—Moose hunter, cook and even boat captain.

1968 Montana Trip

My good buddies Frank Tozser, Bob Hancock, Gene Crawley and Chuck Underwood spent most of the summer of 1968 formulating our dream of a big game hunt to Montana. Gene had made the trip once and kind of guided us through our planning, with stories of finding a big ditch, then throwing rocks down into it and huge mule deer bucks would jump out, like shooting fish in a barrel! How wrong he was!

We applied for and obtained our non-resident licenses, then contacted our outfitter, Art Wycan, who had his ranch just out of Augusta. He had our elk hunt scheduled to hunt in the Bob Marshall Wilderness Area. Gene drove his truck because he had a one hundred gallon gas tank mounted in the bed of his pickup which cut down on our number of stops. Gene started driving and about every 100 miles we would shift drivers, that way none of us got tired driving. We took the ferry across Lake Michigan which also cut down the miles and driving time. We picked up Bob and Chuck at the Augusta, Montana Airport near our destination and finally arrived at Art's ranch.

We all checked our rifles at both stationary targets and also on tires with cardboard that they rolled down the hill to simulate an animal running. Gene was hunting with a .357 Smith & Wesson hand gun with about a nine-inch barrel. He was a real heavy man not in too good of shape and had had a heart attack a little over a year before our hunt. After a great dinner we crawled into our sacks and collapsed!

We were awakened long before daylight. We had breakfast and went down to the corral where Art and his other guide had all the pack horses loaded and we were each given a horse to ride. I will never forget Cobber, a buckskin horse that was very trail wise. They picked out a great big mule for Gene to ride due to his size and also that the gait of a mule was easier on the rider. Remember, none of us had ridden a horse for many years!

As it was breaking day we started out and Art's wife, Edythe, had gone ahead of us all alone with the pack train of horses who were carrying all our gear and groceries, etc., that we would need for a week in the mountains. This is gorgeous country and they only let so many camps in there at a time. Nothing mechanical like chain saws or generators are allowed. You bring back into camp your lunch garbage, beer or pop cans and if you smoke you have to field strip the butts. It is really nice, you see no trash all during the entire trip. We would stop occasionally for pit stops and lunch, otherwise it was go-go-go.

Up and up we went and at about 1 PM we saw Edythe and the pack horses about three miles across a big canyon. They looked like little toys moving along due to the long distance between us. We were going along on a trail not over eight to ten feet across. There were sheer mountains on our right and looking over the edge on our left, the pine trees looked like a lawn it was so far down!

The five of us in our saddles all leaned over to our right, not wanting to look over the trail. At one spot our horses started getting excited and Art told us later they must have smelled a grizzly bear. Two of our pack horses went over the side of the trail. I will never forget seeing them tumbling down the mountainside into the valley below.

Later in the afternoon it started to snow and Art informed us we had just crossed the Continental Divide. We traveled all day long and finally just about dark we made it into the base camp. There were several nice big tents for sleeping, a cook tent, supply tent and a big corral for the horses. Art's wife, Edythe, was our cook and she had a real good supper ready when we arrived. We were stiff as old billy goats from our long ride and we were really hungry. We needed no rocking that night!

For some reason or another Art wanted me to shoot a nice trophy bull he had been watching, so we all went to the spot to wait for the bull. Sure enough out walked several cows into the meadow. Shortly after we began watching, out walked this beautiful bull. It was a 6x6 with a great set of antlers and was only about 100 yards away from us.

I rested my rifle on a big rock and squeezed the trigger, expecting the elk to drop in its tracks. My shot hit a rock way above the bull and to the right. I took two more quick shots as the animals all scattered for cover. We were all dumbfounded. This couldn't happen to me, but it did. When we got back to camp one of the wranglers said, "Oh yeah, I was going to tell you to check your gun as it was on a pack horse that bumped against a tree on the way up."

This guy doesn't realize that the five of us and Art could have killed him for not saying anything about that incident. We took the gun and shot it from a rest and sure enough, the scope had been knocked way off and required several adjustments to bring it back on target. All of us will never forget my missing that beautiful bull and it happened so fast none of them even thought of their own rifles until it was all over.

The next day Bob and his guide Emory shot a 4x4 bull. Bob walked to where it lay and the darned thing jumped up and took off like it had never been shot at all. Bob dropped it for good with another well placed shot. Frank and Art went to a spot and watched a meadow while I made a one man drive down a valley then up to where they were sitting. Several bulls and cows came into the meadow and Frank downed two bulls, a 4x4 and a spike.

The next day was Thanksgiving and we all went out and cut up the three downed elk and brought them into camp and hung all the pieces on the meat pole. Edythe had a delicious Thanksgiving dinner for us—turkey and pies and all the trimmings. She was a real work horse and took care of us as good as any restaurant.

The following day Art positioned me up above the tree line and the other guys were going to try and drive some elk my way. It took an hour to climb where he told me to go. The air was quite thin and it was slow motion to move around. What a gorgeous sight. I was sitting literally on top of the world looking across a great big gorge to a rock formation they called The Chinese Wall. It really humbled me and made me feel very insignificant, like a grain of sand.

I had only sat for about half an hour when I heard a noise like small fire crackers going off until I realized it was the guys making the drive shooting in the air to move some elk. As I watched the woods way down the mountain I saw some movement and saw what appeared to be a bunch of animals that looked like dogs coming out of the timber and headed up the snow covered mountain toward me.

I was told, if I get a chance, to shoot anything as they wanted winter meat and had licenses to cover anything. The elk were in no hurry and kept climbing towards me. They would disappear and then came into sight as they moved kitty corner from my position. Finally, it looked like they were going to cross right over the tip of the mountain, so I decided to see if I could hit one or not.

They were too far away to see if they were bulls or cows, so the next time they came into view I shot about five shots and just kept elevating my gun until one dropped. I reloaded and shot another six shots and then they were gone. I climbed up farther to see what I might have hit and came to a flat spot where I could see the gang of guys that had come out of the woods below me. They looked like toy soldiers they were so far away.

Right on the edge of the flat spot looking down the mountain was a big cow elk that I had hit once. I rested my rifle on the rocks and shot her in the neck. That darn elk fell forward over the edge and went just like a toboggan down very close to where our gang was waiting.

I climbed over the ridge and began tracking the rest of the elk and found some blood on the snow and farther on lay a really nice spike bull. I gutted it out, then noticed that a blood trail was still going away from the bull I had just dressed out. Naturally, I followed this maybe 150 yards or so and there was another nice spike bull deader than a smelt.

Just as I was finishing dressing the second bull here came Emory, one of the guides, and another trail hand and three horses. Boy was I ever glad to see them. They tied ropes to the two bulls and slid the animals through the snow right back to the base camp where they were cut up along with the cow and hung on the meat poles. We had a good celebration that night, then we hit the sack.

I forgot to mention that the two pack horses that went over the mountainside were found by our wranglers the next morning and by all appearances they were OK as was the gear that they were carrying. We could not believe it but it's the Gospel Truth.

Our last night in camp it snowed again and a grizzly bear came to visit and walked off with one of our bags of meat. After looking at the size of the tracks we all agreed that we were not going to tangle with that rascal and that he could have the meat as our treat!

The trip back out was really a beautiful sight to see. The good Lord's handiwork was all around us. We could look back and see all the horses and mules loaded with meat and gear—it was a sight to remember forever. We were used to our horses by now and just dropped the reins and let them follow as they wanted to. After getting back safely to the base camp we spent our last night in camp, then in the morning we loaded up our truck and U-Haul trailer that we had rented back in Augusta. We left our meat to be processed and wrapped and headed out about 100 miles to hunt for antelope.

Gene had made arrangements with a rancher so we could hunt his ranch. We spent the night in a nice motel and had the luxury of a shower and a real bed. Boy, that was most welcome! Early the next morning we had breakfast and headed for the ranch. It was mostly rolling land loaded with sagebrush, a few trees and several watering tanks with windmills. We hunted from the pickup, and Frank and I were the first to get shots. We shot together and were lucky to kill two nice bucks. Gene shot one with his hand gun and Chuck also shot an average size buck.

Those antelope you either kill with the first shot or it may take a box of ammunition before you hit one. I swear that every time you shoot and miss they seem to squat a little lower and shift into a faster gear. They don't seem to jump fences, rather they run full tilt to the fence then turn and run along the fence or turn and run back to where they came from.

Bob would not shoot at the average buck and said he was holding out for a trophy. He had lots of chances but would not shoot. Finally, we came upon a small herd of about a dozen antelope and one was a real nice buck. By the time Bob got out of the truck the animals were running. He emptied his gun and never touched a hair. The darn things ran up to a fence, stopped and came right back across from us, just like in a shooting gallery.

Bob, in a hurry to put another clip in his gun, somehow cut his hand pretty badly on the edge of his clip—but when that big buck led his herd across us for the second time Bob started blasting away and on his last shot of the second clip he knocked down an animal. When we went to dress out the kill it was a DOE! Boy did we razz him about his trophy! We made him keep the doe and when we took our five animals to be processed he talked the meat cutter out of a set of horns, or bought them, to bring home to hang on the wall.

Gene had a friend who had a small Cessna airplane and flew him around to show him the location of some small ponds that had ducks on them and when he got back we took our shotguns and went duck hunting. We would sneak up to the ponds and jump shoot as they flew away. We killed several nice mallards which we cleaned and froze.

Our next outing was a trout trip to a so called lake which turned out to be nothing but a large pond to us, and didn't have even one tree or bush around it. The locals told us to use little marshmallows on our hooks and I'll be darned if it didn't work. We got one of the restaurants that we were patronizing to cook up our trout for supper and they were really delicious. We stayed another couple of days and finally we all shot reasonably good white tail deer, but we missed several shots as the deer were much farther away than they appeared to be.

We drove back to Augusta, and put Bob and Chuck on a plane to fly home. Then we picked up our U-Haul trailer and processed elk, which was packed with dry ice, with a big heavy canvas covering all the meat. The trailer was a good sized trailer with sides and a top on it which worked very well. We stopped on our way home to pick up our deer and antelope and then headed back north and east to good old Gaylord, Michigan.

It is hard to realize this, but don't forget this was in the fall of 1968. This fantastic trip took us about three weeks. Including licenses, food, lodging, guide fees, and gas, everything cost us just a little more than $700 each. A trip like that today would cost close to $10,000 a man.

As I sit here in our family room watching the squirrels and birds at our feeders reminiscing about our great adventure, it seems only a short time ago. Frank and I were visiting the other day and we thought about Chuck, Gene, and Bob who have all gone to the Heavenly Happy Hunting Ground, leaving only Frank and I out of the group to remember.

Another hunt of a lifetime. Fall 1968.

1990 Montana Trip

My good friend, Bob Caras asked me to go to Montana on a combination mule deer and elk hunt along with four other of Bob's friends who had gone as a group before to the Hay Hook Ranch which is just north of Livingston a few miles. This is a big ranch and it had an old abandoned house with no lights, no water, and was way out from the main ranch house.

Three of the group had driven out several days ahead of us, which left Bob, another friend, and I to drive out and meet them. I drove down to Bob's home and spent the night with him, his wife and two darling daughters. We were up very early and packed our gear in Bob's new Suburban. We hooked up his trailer and four wheel ATV, picked up the other hunter and we were finally off to Montana.

We arrived two days later and after meeting our hosts

we drove to the old abandoned farm house and made ourselves comfortable. We had one day before our hunt so Bob drove me around the area we were to hunt. There were high hills, valley, meadows and lots of sagebrush areas. We fished in one of the streams and caught some nice cutthroat trout which was part of our supper that night.

There had been another group of hunters before us and the animals were really spooked. Richie, who was the camp cook and kind of the leader of our group, shot a nice bull elk on a ledge down from a high plateau just at dusk. He and his hunting partner crawled down, dressed it out then headed for camp getting back after dark. One of his buddies shot a nice mule deer buck about the same time. He dressed it out and came back in the dark too.

Bob and I had seen a few deer, but no takers so far. We all got up early the next day and went to bring in the two animals. We got where the mule deer was killed and there was nothing there but the skull and antlers and a little bit of hair. The darn coyotes had eaten everything. Our next stop was for the elk, hoping that the coyotes had not eaten it too. The elk was fine, but was laying on a ledge down the steepest slope in Montana, about 150 yards from where we had parked our vehicles.

We used a block and tackle rig to haul the carcass up to another flat spot, then tied the elk to the rear of Bob's four wheeler. The hill was so steep that two of us had to sit on the front of the ATV to stop it from flipping over backwards. With Bob driving the other three men pulled and pushed until we got the elk back to the trucks. From then on it was a piece of cake taking the elk back to camp. There was also an old barn that we hung our game in that worked real well, keeping the weather and critters away from our meat.

Bob Caras and Gray Wolf, Montana, October 1990.

The next day we were driving along and spotted a real nice mule deer buck way up on a hillside and after two or three shots Bob hit the buck, but it moved out of sight. We spent the best part of an hour looking for him, and finally got the critter and it was a beauty. The elk had left our ranch and had gone to higher ground, so we ended up with only the one bull. We saw lots of deer and everyone ended up getting his own buck. So we had lots of meat for our freezers. We had the meat processed and frozen and packed with dry ice for the trip home.

Bob and I had a nice leisurely trip home, stopping at the Little Big Horn Battle Ground and got to see Custer's last stand and a complete story of how it all happened. It was all very interesting.

While coming through the rain in Wisconsin at about 3 AM, I was driving and the biggest whitetail buck I have ever seen jumped in front of the Suburban. I swear he brushed against our right fender. Bob woke up just in time to see him and we both agreed it was the largest rack either one of us had ever seen on any whitetail deer.

It had been a great trip. Beautiful scenery and good company. Who could ask for more? Everyone got home safely and another episode in Gray Wolf's travels was lodged in our memory banks.

1995 Moose Hunt

It appears that the Canadian government, at least in the Province of Ontario, does not want non-resident hunters hunting their majestic moose anymore. We lease an island and have done so for the last thirty years. We have a very comfortable cabin that can sleep eight people, good boats, canoes and outboards. We have an outside enclosed shower and across our little bridge to the mainland we have a flush toilet equipped with a 55 gallon water storage barrel that is filled by a garden hose attached to our water pump on our main dock. I am telling all this to justify my first sentence regarding the Ontario government not wanting non-resident hunters hunting moose.

First of all, you now have to obtain your license from either a drawing or from a licensed camp outfitter. You also have to be housed by the same group. In our case we had to rent an old log cabin that was in poor repair and use his leaky boats and not very reliable outboards. This kind of stuck in our craws, as right down the lake we could have lived in comfort. But this is taboo now.

Our outfitter has ten cabins at his main base and was only able to get two moose tags. Calf licenses can be bought over the counter, but your chances of shooting a calf are pretty slim. In thirty years of moose hunting I have seen only two moose calves.

In the fall of 1995 four of us decided to try a hunt one more time. Frenchie, Denny Wenzel who came all the way from Atlanta, Georgia, and I put our gear in my Suburban and headed out for Five Mile Lake near Chapleau, Ontario. From there we climbed aboard Frank Uhaus' trusty Beaver aircraft and flew about 20 minutes to Nushatogaini Lake and landed at the north end where our rented cabin was.

This cabin belonged to George and Brenda Nixon

All aboard for another moose season. I was 75 on this hunt.

who had their main camp on Megisan Lake which is about six to seven miles as the crow flies due west of our lake. George had been over and cut some wood for our heat source which was an old cast iron space heater. He had cleaned the cabin and put two bottles of champagne on the table for us to celebrate if we lucked out and killed a moose. It really felt strange to go to another cabin on our lake when half way down to the south was our own Shangri-la.

Later on, our fourth member, Chum Noirot, flew in with his Super Cub on floats to hunt with us. Chum lives across Otsego Lake from our home and his place is where we kept our float plane for many years. We cleaned out a place down by George's boat house where we could tie the plane up out of the wind. Then we commenced to make ourselves as comfortable as possible in our quarters for the next week.

We had arrived one day ahead of the non-resident hunting season so we spent most of the day checking for sign and picking our spots to hunt. Frenchie was to hunt with me on a creek that flowed into our lake and he could watch a big pond and the river. I would go to the north end of the creek and I would watch a grassy area and part of the creek, about a half mile from Frenchie.

Chum and Denny were to hunt a big pond right across the lake from our cabin. We call this area Emil's Pond, and Chum was to hunt the southwest area and Denny the northeast end. On our way out that afternoon we came within fifty yards of a nice big cow and we got some good pictures and were eagerly awaiting the next day in hopes to see that cow again.

We were up before daylight and after a hearty breakfast we packed lunches and headed for our respective spots. I dropped Frenchie off at the point, and paddled up the creek to where I was going to spend the day. I had picked a spot where I could watch the meadow and about 150 yards of the creek. I had made a nest at the bottom of a spruce tree which was my backrest, and with a thick layer of spruce boughs and a boat cushion I could get down in the marsh grass and watch everything!

It was just breaking day and what a gorgeous one it was. As the sun came up a beaver swam by and went up to check his dam, some geese flew over heading south, a couple of ravens went squawking by, every once in a while a woodpecker would hammer away on a tree, and I was really starting to enjoy the warmth of the sun as it climbed above the trees. I poured myself a cup of coffee and had a half a sandwich and a cookie and pulled out a pocket Western to read.

Shortly before 11 AM, I was sure I had heard a stick break across the creek in a large area of black spruce but it was not repeated. Just the same I put down my book, picked up my rifle and laid it across my lap just in case! Shortly after I heard a sucking sort of noise and I knew that I was about to have company. Sure enough, across the creek I picked up the movement of a nice cow which was moving parallel to me through the spruce trees heading down river.

It was about a hundred yards away broadside, but it was hard to pick a good spot through the trees. I shot once and the ol' girl moved into high gear and I shot three more times and I know that I had killed at least two trees and had hit the moose once. However, it kept running and jumped into the creek and just as she came out on my side I shot my fifth time and the moose dropped back into the creek and thoroughly anchored herself in the bog. I waited a few minutes, loaded my gear into the boat and paddled down stream to where the moose lay in the loon s--t as we called it.

I put the motor on the boat and went to pick up Frenchie who was anxiously waiting to see what all the shooting was about. We picked up his gear and headed back to the moose. Both of her front legs were mired in the mud and we could not budge it at all, so I dug a rope out from my pack and tied it around the head and used the outboard to try to wiggle the legs loose. All to no avail. We were about to go to our own cabin to get our block and tackle when Chum and Denny showed up thinking that we probably had several moose down with five shots fired.

We hooked both boats to the rope and finally pried my big cow loose and out in the middle of the creek. We

Chum and Gray Wolf with cow in tow.

towed the moose out of Brandenberg Creek across our lake to a nice big flat rock, where our original tent camp was. We gutted out the critter and went to our boat house for the block and tackle. It was all the four of us could do to hang the moose from some birch trees so the carcass would cool out over night, making it ready to cut up and hang it on our meat pole.

Chum and Denny went back to Emil's Pond for the evening hunt. Frenchie and I went back to the cabin to make supper. Moose tenderloins with all the trimmings were on the menu. Frenchie was a real good cook and dearly loved doing it too!

About 5 PM just as it was getting dark we heard a single shot. Out came the bottles of champagne waiting for our two hunters to show up. In about an hour we heard their motor and it was pitch dark out by now. Denny was all excited and said that just before dark a young bull had come out of the spruce trees and walked out in the marsh grass to the creek. He shot and the moose ran across the marsh and went out of his range of vision. We all had a glass of champagne and sat down to a wonderful supper of the moose tenderloins that Frenchie had prepared for us.

After supper we talked over the situation and not wanting the moose to spoil, Chum, Denny and I went back to Emil's Pond. We took the canoe across the pond and up a small creek that took us within 100 yards of Denny's moose that was laying dead near the southeast corner of the pond. It did not take us long to dress out the moose and prop open the cavity so that the meat would cool properly. It was now about 10:30 PM. When we got back to camp Frenchie heard us coming so he

Up close and personal with a nice cow moose the day before the season opened.

had Hot Toddies made for us. Needless to say we climbed into our sleeping bags and literally died.

The next morning Frenchie and I went down to my moose and proceeded to cut it up and bag it in stockinette. Chum and Denny did the same with Denny's moose and we met at the cabin early in the afternoon, had lunch and went back to my moose. We loaded all the bags into the boat and Frenchie took the boatload of meat while Denny, Chum and I went and cut up Denny's moose. It was a lot of hard work, and we had to haul all the meat from Emil's Pond to our lake across the portage which is about a quarter of a mile of packing.

Both Denny and Chum made the remark, "Boy, if I had known it was this much work I never would have shot the dang moose." We finally got all the meat out of the boat and hauled it back to the cabin. Frenchie again had our supper all ready and after a good meal we forgot all about the ordeal we had just gone through.

The next couple of days, we spent resting, reading, and fishing. Frank flew in and took out our moose meat, then came back and picked up Frenchie, Denny, myself and all the gear. Chum loaded up his Super Cub and flew home to Gaylord. We drove back home with lots of memories.

I do believe that this trip was to be my last moose hunting trip unless they change the laws for non-residents. My record still stands—30 years hunting moose and 33 kills. Not too shabby for the Old Gray Wolf! Within two years after this last hunt, both Frenchie and Denny lost their battles with cancer and both are now fishing and hunting in the Heavenlies!

Heave-Ho! Chum, Frenchie and Gray Wolf.

Gray Wolf's last moose—number 33. Nushatogaini 1995.

Farewell

Old Gray Wolf will soon be 82 years old. I walk a little slower due to a complete knee replacement a few short years ago, but my mind is sharp and I still put in 40 to 50 hours at the Sport Shop and at our Real Estate company. I still ice fish nearly every week in the winter, make at least three trips to our Shangri-la in Canada each year, and spend quite a bit of time working at the deer camp. I keep our freezer full of venison, fish and wild turkey and plan to do this as long as the good Lord will let me. It is said that the time you spend hunting and fishing is not counted against your life span, so the Old Lobo should live to be 220 years old!

I have travelled by land, sea, and air, but I have also taken time to be a loving father to our children and my dear partner in life, Edythe. We have been married for

59 years now and are still very much in love with each other.

I feel I have been richly rewarded by God who has looked after me all during my life and blessed me and my family through many trials and tribulations. It saddens my heart to see the way our country has slipped in the last 30 to 40 years in their beliefs and values. Hopefully they will return prayer in our schools and put God back in government to make decisions for the betterment of the people and not to feather their own nests.

I hope you have enjoyed reading and sharing my adventures as much as I have enjoyed relating them to you and may God bless all of you.

— Gray Wolf

ABOUT THE AUTHOR

Don Butcher is a Past Master of the VFW Post #1407, a Life Member of the Disabled Veterans, and member of The American Legion. He has served on the Gaylord Board of Education, and is a past President of the Otsego Lake Chamber of Commerce, as well as the local Sportsman's Club, and was Sportsman of the Year.

He is also a past President of the Gaylord Rotary Club. He was co-organizer and past President of The Alpine Snowmobile Trails Association, and one of the original organizers of the Winterfest. He served on the Otsego County Road Commission for 31 years and also on the Bagley Township Board of Review.

Don is a devout Christian, belongs to the Christian Coalition, Masons, Shriners and is a member of The Eagles Club and the NRA. The Gray Wolf has left his tracks on all of the above and many other people and places. He and his wife Edythe live in Gaylord, Michigan.